Reader's Digest
Fast Food

Reader's Digest
Fast Food

Published by The Reader's Digest Association Limited
London • New York • Sydney • Montreal

Fast Food is part of a series of cookery books called
Eat Well Live Well and was created by Amazon Publishing Limited.

Series Editor *Norma MacMillan*
Volume Editor *Felicity Jackson*
Art Director *Ruth Prentice*
Photographic Direction *Ruth Prentice, Alison Shackleton*
DTP *Peter Howard*
Editorial Assistant *Jasmine Brown*
Nutritionist *Fiona Hunter, BSc Hons (Nutri.), Dip. Dietetics*

Contributors
Writers *Sara Buenfeld, Carole Clements, Linda Collister,
Beverly LeBlanc, Sara Lewis, Janette Marshall, Maggie Mayhew,
Kate Moseley, Maggie Pannell, Marlena Spieler*
Recipe Testers *Anna Brandenburger, Bridget Colvin,
Emma-Lee Gow, Clare Lewis, Gina Steer, Susanna Tee*
Photographers *Martin Brigdale, Gus Filgate, William Lingwood*
Stylist *Helen Trent*
Home Economists *Jules Beresford, Lucy McKelvie, Lucy Miller,
Bridget Sargeson, Linda Tubby, Sunil Vijayakar*

For Reader's Digest
Project Editor *Rachel Warren Chadd*
Project Art Editor *Louise Turpin*

Reader's Digest General Books
Editorial Director *Cortina Butler*
Art Director *Nick Clark*

First Edition Copyright © 2001
The Reader's Digest Association Limited
11 Westferry Circus, Canary Wharf, London E14 4HE
www.readersdigest.co.uk

Paperback edition 2003
Paperback Art Editor *Jane McKenna*

ISBN 0 276 42798 X

Notes for the reader
• Use all metric or all imperial measures when preparing a recipe,
as the two sets of measurements are not exact equivalents.
• Recipes were tested using metric measures and conventional
(not fan-assisted) ovens. Medium eggs were used, unless
otherwise specified.
• Can sizes are approximate, as weights can vary slightly
according to the manufacturer.
• Preparation and cooking times are only intended as a guide.

The nutritional information in this book is for reference only.
The editors urge anyone with continuing medical problems or
symptoms to consult a doctor.

Contents

Eating well to live well

Eating a healthy diet can help you look good, feel great and have lots of energy. Nutrition fads come and go, but the simple keys to eating well remain the same: enjoy a variety of food – no single food contains all the vitamins, minerals, fibre and other essential components you need for health and vitality – and get the balance right by looking at the proportions of the different foods you eat. Add some regular exercise too – at least 30 minutes a day, 3 times a week – and you'll be helping yourself to live well and make the most of your true potential.

Getting it into proportion

Current guidelines are that most people in the UK should eat more starchy foods, more fruit and vegetables, and less fat, meat products and sugary foods. It is almost impossible to give exact amounts that you should eat, as every single person's requirements vary, depending on size, age and the amount of energy expended during the day. However, nutrition experts have suggested an ideal balance of the different foods that provide us with energy (calories) and the nutrients needed for health. The number of daily portions of each of the food groups will vary from person to person – for example, an active teenager might need to eat up to 14 portions of starchy carbohydrates every day, whereas a sedentary adult would only require 6 or 7 portions – but the proportions of the food groups in relation to each other should ideally stay the same.

More detailed explanations of food groups and nutritional terms can be found on pages 156–158, together with brief guidelines on amounts which can be used in conjunction with the nutritional analyses of the recipes. A simple way to get the balance right, however, is to imagine a daily 'plate' divided into the different food groups. On the imaginary 'plate', starchy carbohydrates fill at least one-third of the space, thus constituting the main part of your meals. Fruit and vegetables fill the same amount of space. The remaining third of the 'plate' is divided mainly between protein foods and dairy foods, with just a little space allowed for foods containing fat and sugar. These are the proportions to aim for.

It isn't essential to eat the ideal proportions on the 'plate' at every meal, or even every day – balancing them over a week or two is just as good. The healthiest diet for you and your family is one that is generally balanced and sustainable in the long term.

Our daily plate

Starchy carbohydrate foods: eat 6–14 portions a day
At least 50% of the calories in a healthy diet should come from carbohydrates, and most of that from starchy foods – bread, potatoes and other starchy vegetables, pasta, rice and cereals. For most people in the UK this means doubling current intake. Starchy carbohydrates are the best foods for energy. They also provide protein and essential vitamins and minerals, particularly those from the B group. Eat a variety of starchy foods, choosing wholemeal or wholegrain types whenever possible, because the fibre they contain helps to prevent constipation, bowel disease, heart disease and other health problems.
What is a portion of starchy foods?
Some examples are: 3 tbsp breakfast cereal • 2 tbsp muesli • 1 slice of bread or toast • 1 bread roll, bap or bun • 1 small pitta bread, naan bread or chapatti • 3 crackers or crispbreads • 1 medium-sized potato • 1 medium-sized plantain or small sweet potato • 2 heaped tbsp boiled rice • 2 heaped tbsp boiled pasta.

Fruit and vegetables: eat at least 5 portions a day
Nutrition experts are unanimous that we would all benefit from eating more fruit and vegetables each day – a total of at least 400 g (14 oz) of fruit and vegetables (edible part) is the target. Fruit and vegetables provide vitamin C for immunity and healing, and other 'antioxidant' vitamins and minerals for protection against cardiovascular disease and cancer. They also offer several 'phytochemicals' that help protect against cancer, and B vitamins, especially folate, which is important for women planning a pregnancy, to prevent birth defects. All of these, plus other nutrients, work together to boost well-being.

Antioxidant nutrients (e.g. vitamins C and beta-carotene, which are mainly derived from fruit and vegetables) and vitamin E help to prevent harmful free radicals in the body initiating or accelerating cancer, heart disease, cataracts, arthritis, general ageing, sun damage to skin, and damage to sperm. Free radicals occur naturally as a by-product of normal cell function, but are also caused by pollutants such as tobacco smoke and over-exposure to sunlight.
What is a portion of fruit or vegetables?
Some examples are: 1 medium-sized portion of vegetables or salad • 1 medium-sized piece of fresh fruit • 6 tbsp (about 140 g/5 oz) stewed or canned fruit • 1 small glass (100 ml/3½ fl oz) fruit juice.

Dairy foods: eat 2–3 portions a day
Dairy foods, such as milk, cheese, yogurt and fromage frais, are the best source of calcium for strong bones and teeth, and important for the nervous system. They also provide some protein for growth and repair, vitamin B_{12}, and vitamin A for healthy eyes. They are particularly valuable foods for young children, who need full-fat versions at least up to age 2. Dairy foods are also especially important for adolescent girls to prevent the development of osteoporosis later in life, and for women throughout life generally.

To limit fat intake, wherever possible adults should choose lower-fat dairy foods, such as semi-skimmed milk and low-fat yogurt.
What is a portion of dairy foods?
Some examples are: 1 medium-sized glass (200 ml/7 fl oz) milk • 1 matchbox-sized piece (40 g/1½ oz) Cheddar cheese • 1 small pot of yogurt • 125 g (4½ oz) cottage cheese or fromage frais.

Protein foods: eat 2–4 portions a day

Lean meat, fish, eggs and vegetarian alternatives provide protein for growth and cell repair, as well as iron to prevent anaemia. Meat also provides B vitamins for healthy nerves and digestion, especially vitamin B_{12}, and zinc for growth and healthy bones and skin. Only moderate amounts of these protein-rich foods are required. An adult woman needs about 45 g of protein a day and an adult man 55 g, which constitutes about 11% of a day's calories. This is less than the current average intake. For optimum health, we need to eat some protein every day.

What is a portion of protein-rich food?

Some examples are: 3 slices (85–100 g/3–3½ oz) of roast beef, pork, ham, lamb or chicken • about 100 g (3½ oz) grilled offal • 115–140 g (4–5 oz) cooked fillet of white or oily fish (not fried in batter) • 3 fish fingers • 2 eggs (up to 7 a week) • about 140 g/5 oz baked beans • 60 g (2¼ oz) nuts, peanut butter or other nut products.

Foods containing fat: 1–5 portions a day

Unlike fruit, vegetables and starchy carbohydrates, which can be eaten in abundance, fatty foods should not exceed 33% of the day's calories in a balanced diet, and only 10% of this should be from saturated fat. This quantity of fat may seem a lot, but it isn't – fat contains more than twice as many calories per gram as either carbohydrate or protein.

Overconsumption of fat is a major cause of weight and health problems. A healthy diet must contain a certain amount of fat to provide fat-soluble vitamins and essential fatty acids, needed for the development and function of the brain, eyes and nervous system, but we only need a small amount each day – just 25 g is required, which is much less than we consume in our Western diet. The current recommendations from the Department of Health are a maximum of 71 g fat (of this, 21.5 g saturated) for women each day and 93.5 g fat (28.5 g saturated) for men. The best sources of the essential fatty acids are natural fish oils and pure vegetable oils.

What is a portion of fatty foods?

Some examples are: 1 tsp butter or margarine • 2 tsp low-fat spread • 1 tsp cooking oil • 1 tbsp mayonnaise or vinaigrette (salad dressing) • 1 tbsp cream • 1 individual packet of crisps.

Foods containing sugar: 0–2 portions a day

Although many foods naturally contain sugars (e.g. fruit contains fructose, milk lactose), health experts recommend that we limit 'added' sugars. Added sugars, such as table sugar, provide only calories – they contain no vitamins, minerals or fibre to contribute to health, and it is not necessary to eat them at all. But, as the old adage goes, 'a little of what you fancy does you good' and sugar is no exception. Denial of foods, or using them as rewards or punishment, is not a healthy attitude to eating, and can lead to cravings, binges and yo-yo dieting. Sweet foods are a pleasurable part of a well-balanced diet, but added sugars should account for no more than 11% of the total daily carbohydrate intake.

In assessing how much sugar you consume, don't forget that it is a major ingredient of many processed and ready-prepared foods.

What is a portion of sugary foods?

Some examples are: 3 tsp sugar • 1 heaped tsp jam or honey • 2 biscuits • half a slice of cake • 1 doughnut • 1 Danish pastry • 1 small bar of chocolate • 1 small tube or bag of sweets.

Too salty

Salt (sodium chloride) is essential for a variety of body functions, but we tend to eat too much through consumption of salty processed foods, 'fast' foods and ready-prepared foods, and by adding salt in cooking and at the table. The end result can be rising blood pressure as we get older, which puts us at higher risk of heart disease and stroke. Eating more vegetables and fruit increases potassium intake, which can help to counteract the damaging effects of salt.

Alcohol in a healthy diet

In recent research, moderate drinking of alcohol has been linked with a reduced risk of heart disease and stroke among men and women over 45. However, because of other risks associated with alcohol, particularly in excessive quantities, no doctor would recommend taking up drinking if you are teetotal. The healthiest pattern of drinking is to enjoy small amounts of alcohol with food, to have alcohol-free days and always to avoid getting drunk. A well-balanced diet is vital because nutrients from food (vitamins and minerals) are needed to detoxify the alcohol.

Water – the best choice

Drinking plenty of non-alcoholic liquid each day is an often overlooked part of a well-balanced diet. A minimum of 8 glasses (which is about 2 litres/3½ pints) is the ideal. If possible, these should not all be tea or coffee, as these are stimulants and diuretics, which cause the body to lose liquids, taking with them water-soluble vitamins. Water is the best choice. Other good choices are fruit or herb teas or tisanes, fruit juices – diluted with water, if preferred – or semi-skimmed milk (full-fat milk for very young children). Fizzy sugary or acidic drinks such as cola are more likely to damage tooth enamel than other drinks.

As a guide to the vitamin and mineral content of foods and recipes in the book, we have used the following terms and symbols, based on the percentage of the daily RNI provided by one serving for the average adult man or woman aged 19–49 years (see also pages 156–158):

✓✓✓   or excellent   at least 50% (half)

✓✓   or good   25–50% (one-quarter to one-half)

✓   or useful   10–25% (one-tenth to one-quarter)

Note that recipes contribute other nutrients, but the analyses only include those that provide at least 10% RNI per portion. Vitamins and minerals where deficiencies are rare are not included.

Ⓥ denotes that a recipe is suitable for vegetarians.

Super Fast Food

Quick and tasty to keep you healthy

Our lives have never been busier. With many people working longer hours, and coping with the demands of active family and social lives, there is less time than ever for preparing food and for cooking. All too often, we just grab a takeaway or ready-made meal. But if we want to look good, feel great and have lots of energy, we need to eat nutritious food most of the time. And the good news is that quick cooking often means healthy cooking, as more nutrients are retained. In this chapter, the basics of good fast food are explained, from how to stock up your kitchen cupboards and what to buy fresh for quick cooking, to useful time-saving methods and tools.

Fast food in a healthy diet

Fast food has become synonymous with junk food, but it doesn't have to be like that – there is no need to sacrifice health for speed. Lots of fresh foods require little or no cooking and with minimum preparation keep more of their natural flavours, giving you fast, tasty and nutritious meals.

Fast and fine

Fast food can play a big part in a healthy well-balanced diet. The recipes in this book are for the occasions when you have little time to spend in the kitchen, but still want something fresh and home-made. They all follow the healthy guidelines of a high proportion of starchy carbohydrate, a moderate amount of protein-rich food and plenty of fruit and vegetables.

• Lots of low-fat, starchy (complex carbohydrate) foods are perfect for fast meals. Breads, pasta, rice, instant polenta, bulghur wheat, couscous and quinoa are all nutritious fast foods that will boost your starchy carbohydrate intake.

• Fruit and vegetables are full of vitamins, minerals, fibre and protective compounds. Many can be eaten raw, while others need only brief cooking.

• Canned pulses, such as kidney, haricot and flageolet beans, chickpeas and lentils, are a good source of B-group vitamins and a cheap source of protein. Despite the canning process, they still retain a valuable nutrient content.

• Lean cuts of meat for stir-frying or grilling, chicken breasts and drumsticks, fish fillets and steaks, shellfish and eggs are all fast-cooking protein-rich foods.

Plan ahead

The key to fast and healthy cooking is to plan ahead, perhaps working out a week's menu all at once, and shopping to make sure everything is to hand when you need it. This may seem an effort to begin with, but it will save you time in the long run. Stock up your storecupboard, fridge and freezer (see pages 16–20), and get into the habit of making enough for 2 meals and freezing half for another occasion. Try to include as wide a variety of foods as possible in your menus, because no single food contains all the vitamins, minerals, fibre and other essential components you need for good health.

Eating little and often

Grazing – having frequent small snacks throughout the day rather than fewer large meals – is a good way to maintain energy levels, as long as the snacks are healthy ones. Delicious, home-made snacks made from wholesome ingredients can increase the intake of vital nutrients and can be prepared in anything from 5 to 30 minutes – often quicker than it would be to order and collect a take-away.

Healthier choices for take-aways

Most of us eat take-aways from time to time, and nowadays it is possible to buy much healthier snacks and meals than the traditional burger, doner kebab, fried chicken, or fish and chips. Lots of snack bars offer sandwiches on a variety of delicious breads, simply bursting with salad or vegetable accompaniments. Vegetarian meals, pizzas, imaginative salads and even sushi are more available country-wide. Here are some ideas to help you choose the healthier alternatives when you buy a take-away.

• Increase your fibre intake by choosing wholemeal or fibre-enriched bread rather than white bread.

• When choosing a sandwich filling, include salad and opt for lower-fat plain meats such as chicken, beef or ham rather than pâtés, bacon or sausages.

• Stir-fried prawns are much lower in fat than those coated in breadcrumbs or batter and deep-fried.

• Tandoori chicken is lower in fat than a curry or rich sauce.

• Steamed or boiled rice has less than half the calories and fat of special fried rice.

• Shish kebab with salad is much less fatty, and much more nutritious, than doner kebab.

• Thick-crust pizzas offer more starchy carbohydrate than thin ones and they are very satisfying.

super fast food

► In 10 minutes: Banana and apricot smoothie (see page 44) is bursting with vitamin C

►► In 15 minutes: Butter bean dip with crudités offers an ideal balance of nutrients (see page 59)

◄◄ In 30 minutes: Spinach and potato frittata (see page 96) is rich in B vitamins

◄ In 15 minutes: Fruit bread slices (see page 40) will provide a great energy boost

► In 25 minutes: Hoisin beef stir-fry (see page 68) is the perfect special meal-in-a-bowl

►► In 15 minutes: Citrus salad with dates (see page 140) is a fat-free vitamin C-rich dessert

Choosing food for fast cooking

It is perfectly possible to prepare delicious and nutritious meals in a matter of minutes. Simply pick and choose from an enormous choice of fresh foods, following the healthy eating guidelines of plenty of starchy (complex) carbohydrates and vitamin-rich fruit and vegetables, and moderate amounts of protein.

Satisfying starch

In a healthy well-balanced diet, starchy or complex carbohydrate foods should provide at least half of the daily calories. Many starchy foods take little or no time to prepare and so are ideal for fast nutritious meals.

• Bread is the champion starchy fast food, as the base of sandwiches of all kinds and as an instant accompaniment for quick meals. The variety of breads available means you always have plenty of choice.

• Most rice takes just 15–20 minutes to cook, and can be flavoured in the pan to provide a delicious variety of dishes to partner stove-top curries, grilled kebabs and stir-fries.

• Couscous only needs to be soaked in boiling water for a few minutes and then fluffed up with a fork.

• Bulghur wheat takes 15–20 minutes simmering, pasta and instant polenta even less.

• If cut into slices or chunks, potatoes can be cooked in 10 minutes; whole new potatoes need just 15 minutes.

Vital vitamins

Vegetables and fruit are the best sources of vitamin C and beta-carotene, both of which are powerful antioxidants that play a vital role in keeping us healthy. Along with vitamin E, fibre and other protective compounds found in plants, they help to prevent heart disease, strokes, cancer and degenerative diseases like cataracts. Many vegetables, particularly the dark green, leafy types, also supply useful amounts of vitamins from the B group.

To be at their most nutritious, fruit and vegetables must be very fresh – the longer they are 'on the shelf', the more of their vital vitamins will have been lost. They will also lose a lot of their good flavour. Although chilled prepared vegetables are not as rich in nutrients as whole vegetables, they still have something to offer, and they are very convenient.

Shopping for fresh produce should be done on a regular basis, and in a greengrocery or supermarket with a rapid turnover. When it isn't convenient to shop for fresh fruit and

▲ Starchy foods are the basis of satisfying quick meals

▲ Fruit and vegetables add vitamins and minerals

▲ Quick to cook or ready to eat protein-rich foods, such as lean meat, seafood, eggs, cheese, pulses and tofu, make nutritious main meals

vegetables, the next best thing is to use frozen. Produce frozen within hours of being picked will actually contain more vitamins than 'fresh' produce that may be days old before it even reaches the consumer.

Be quick to keep maximum benefits

Fast methods are often the healthiest ways to prepare and cook fruit and vegetables, as more of their nutrients are retained.

● Prepare fruit and vegetables as close to cooking/eating as possible.

● Use unpeeled fruit and vegetables where appropriate – apples, potatoes and courgettes, for example – because much of the vitamin and mineral content is just under the skin. There is also valuable fibre in the skin.

● Tear the leaves of green leafy vegetables rather than cutting them, as tearing releases fewer of the enzymes that destroy vitamins.

● Cook vegetables for the shortest time possible and in the minimum amount of water. Add the vegetables to boiling water, as bringing to the boil in cold water prolongs the cooking time and nutrient loss.

Rich in protein

Meat and poultry are excellent sources of protein, and they provide many vitamins and minerals. The cuts best suited to quick cooking are those that are healthily lean and tender. While some of these are expensive, there is little or no waste, so smaller quantities can be bought.

Protein-rich fish and shellfish also have a lot to offer in a healthy diet. As a bonus, white fish is virtually fat-free, while oily fish is rich in the 'essential' omega-3 fatty acids. All fish and shellfish is very quick to cook, quicker even than most meat and poultry.

● Lamb neck fillet or boneless leg, pork fillet (tenderloin) and beef fillet or other tender steak can be cut into cubes to make kebabs for grilling, diced for quick stove-top curries, cut into thin strips for stir-fries, or minced to make burgers.

● Steaks, pork chops, and lamb chops and cutlets can all be grilled, barbecued or cooked on a ridged cast-iron grill pan. Veal escalopes and very thin 'minute' steaks can be pan-fried.

● Poultry fillets (skinless and boneless breasts), thighs and drumsticks are ideal for grilling, barbecuing and pan-frying.

● Small whole fish such as plaice, sole, trout, herring and mackerel can be grilled or pan-fried. There is no need to add any fat when grilling oil-rich fish, and only a tiny amount is needed for pan-frying.

● Fish fillets and steaks suit just about every quick cooking method. Fillets can also be cut into strips for stir-frying, and steaks can be cut into cubes for kebabs.

● Shellfish such as prawns, scallops and mussels must be cooked quickly to retain their juicy texture.

Other protein sources

● Eggs contain vitamins A, B_2, B_{12}, E and niacin, and iron.

● Tofu is a low-fat protein food made from soya. A source of calcium, it may also play a part in preventing heart disease.

● Cheese is a valuable source of calcium, zinc, phosphorus, niacin and vitamin B_{12}.

● Canned pulses (beans and lentils) are a convenient source of protein when you are short of time.

Fast cooking methods

The healthiest cooking methods cook fresh food quickly but thoroughly in the minimum amount of fat or water, thus reducing vitamin and mineral losses and avoiding the addition of unnecessary saturated fat and calories. Not only that – you'll find these are the most delicious ways to prepare food too!

Quick as a flash in the pan

All the cooking methods below will produce nutritious food, full of delicious flavour, in a matter of minutes.

Steaming is a very healthy way of cooking vegetables – there is less loss of the B and C vitamin content than with boiling, which can destroy 40–70% of vitamin C. Delicate poultry and fish dishes that would not withstand the rigours of the barbecue or grill are also well suited to steaming. Water is boiled beneath a trivet or a basket in a wok or saucepan, or special steamer. The food is placed above the water in a perforated container through which the steam passes to cook it.

Stir-frying produces tender meat and crisp vegetables in a very short time, retaining the maximum vitamin content.

If there is time, it's good to marinate the meat first for 10 minutes or so, to add extra flavour. Traditionally, stir-frying is done in a wok. The round base and deep sloping sides conduct heat evenly over the wok's surface, helping to cook food quickly over a high heat. Food can be cooked in little or no fat because it is in the wok for such a short time and is constantly being stirred, so it doesn't have a chance to stick to the pan. Move the food with long wooden chopsticks, a wok scoop or a wooden spatula.

Grilling can be done without the addition of fat. White fish can be drizzled with lemon juice and sprinkled with seasoning or herbs. Use a moderate heat as high heat will dry out and scorch delicate fish. Marinate meat for kebabs in a mixture of herbs and wine, stock or low-fat yogurt for a few minutes to flavour and moisten it, then grill on a rack so that excess fat drains away and can be discarded.

Griddled food is cooked on a ridged pan on the hob in the same way that hot flat stones were used for cooking meat, fish and flat breads in more primitive cultures. This method sears food quickly, giving rich flavour and colour, and the ridges produce

Time-saving microwave techniques

Microwave cooking has some health and time advantages:

• Vegetables and fruit can be cooked quickly in a covered dish without any extra liquid. Loss of water-soluble and heat-sensitive vitamins can thus be kept to a minimum.

• Creamy porridge can be made in 2 minutes in a bowl, avoiding a messy saucepan to wash, and providing a nourishing quick breakfast.

• Fish cooks very quickly in the microwave, and doesn't dry out, so no fat is needed.

• Many sauces can be made in their serving jugs to save time and washing up. The home-made versions are much more nutritious than cartons of custard and other sauces that are high in fat and/or sugar and that contain thickeners and other additives.

• Combination microwave ovens, which combine conventional heat with microwaves, are the most effective at saving time and producing good results. For example, baked potatoes with crisp skins can be produced in 10–15 minutes. Alternatively, you can use the microwave in combination with your conventional oven to bake potatoes in just 20 minutes. Turn the oven on to heat to 200ºC (400ºF, gas mark 6), then put your potatoes in the microwave to cook for 10 minutes. Transfer the potatoes to the hot oven and crisp up for 10 minutes.

an attractive striped effect. If the pan is very hot and there is natural oil in the food – oily fish, for example – it can often be cooked without any fat at all, otherwise a light brushing of oil may be needed to prevent sticking.

En papillote is a method of cooking food tightly sealed in a baking parchment or foil parcel in the oven. It is a good way to cook whole fish, fish fillets or lean cuts of meat that might otherwise dry out in the oven heat or disintegrate on the grill.

Healthy fast cooking methods

► Stir-frying uses the minimum of fat: Tofu and vegetable stir-fry (see page 90)

▼ Steaming retains water-soluble vitamins: Steamed sea bass fillets with spring vegetables (see page 118)

▲ Baking *en papillote* keeps in all the nutritious juices: Hot fruity parcels (see page 147)

◄ Grilling needs no fat at all: Greek lamb kebabs (see page 72)

Stocking up for fast cooking

To prepare food quickly, both cook and kitchen need to be well organised, with the kitchen equipped for ease of use and stocked with a good selection of foods that you can take out when you need to whip up a fast meal.

In the storecupboard

Lots of nutritious foods come conveniently ready-prepared in cans and jars, and they are perfect for the busy cook. These stand-by foods, along with packet foods, can provide meals by themselves or be combined with fresh foods, bought regularly, to produce delicious quick dishes.

Canned staples

Canned foods can play an important part in healthy fast meals.

Fish such as salmon, tuna, sardines, pilchards and herring are good sources of protein. Choose varieties canned in water to cut out the calories in oil or the sodium in brine. Fish bones, which are made edible by the canning process, are an excellent source of calcium – a medium-sized portion (about 100 g/3½ oz) of canned sardines will provide 78% of the recommended daily amount of calcium for women aged 19–49. Canning reduces the valuable omega-3 content of oily fish – salmon, which has a higher content to start with, loses

less in the canning process than tuna. So to be sure of getting enough of this essential fatty acid it is important to eat some fresh oily fish as well as canned on a regular basis.

Pulses, such as lentils, chickpeas and kidney, haricot and butter beans, are rich in soluble fibre and vitamins. They make an excellent basis for all sorts of fast meals. Before using, drain and rinse well to get rid of salt and sugar in the canning liquid. Baked (haricot) beans are available without sugar and salt in the tomato sauce.

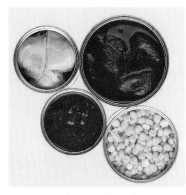

Sweetcorn kernels are a good source of fibre and beta-carotene, and can be fresher than corn-on-the-cob (unless it is picked and cooked straight from the garden). Look for versions that are canned without sugar and salt.

Tomatoes contain lycopene, a carotenoid compound that acts as an antioxidant and is believed to be a valuable anti-cancer agent. The lycopene in tomatoes is made more available to the

body when tomatoes are cooked, so canned tomatoes (and tomato purée and passata) are a better source of lycopene than fresh tomatoes. Canned tomatoes are available whole or chopped.

Bamboo shoots and water chestnuts are convenient crunchy ingredients that can add interest to Oriental stir-fries.

Fruits such as apricots, pineapple, pears and peaches are useful stand-bys for quick puddings.

Although containing less vitamin C than fresh fruit, they still contribute valuable amounts, and apricots are a good source of beta-carotene. Choose varieties canned in natural juice or water, as syrup contains a lot of sugar.

Packets and boxes

Dried pasta in all shapes and sizes is an indispensable healthy storecupboard food. Low in fat and high in complex carbohydrates, it cooks in less than 15 minutes, to make nutritious quick meals. Oriental noodles, such as Chinese rice and egg noodles, only need soaking in boiling water or very brief cooking.

Bulghur wheat is partially cooked crushed wheat grains. It is deliciously chewy, and can be used like rice in salads, pilafs and many other dishes.

Couscous, made from rolled semolina, is served in much the same way as rice and pasta, particularly to partner stews.

Polenta (pre-cooked maize or corn meal) is available in quick-cooking versions, or ready-made in a roll that simply needs to be sliced and heated.

Quinoa is an ancient grain that was used by the Incas. It is rich in nutrients with a high amino acid content. It is cooked like rice and can be used in the same way.

Rice is wonderfully versatile, and there are many types to choose from. Most can be cooked quickly, while others, such as nutritious brown rice, take about 30 minutes.

Lentils, unlike other pulses, do not need to be soaked before cooking. Split red lentils and yellow ones cook in about 15 minutes (any longer and they turn into a purée).

Ready-to-eat dried fruits, such as apricots and mango, make a handy energy-rich snack and they can be added to breakfast cereals, salads and quick puddings.

Nuts are a source of vitamin E, folate, phytochemicals and protein, and they provide useful amounts of the minerals iron, selenium and zinc. Their high oil content is mainly beneficial polyunsaturated fatty acids, so they can make a nutritious contribution to many dishes.

Seeds such as sunflower and pumpkin are a good source of essential fatty acids and minerals. They can be toasted in a dry pan or under the grill to make a tasty addition to salads and sandwich fillings or a snack on their own.

Breakfast cereals make perfect fast snacks at any time of day and they are a good source of vitamins and minerals. Choose those that are unsweetened or sweetened naturally with fruit rather than with sugar.

Crispbreads, rice cakes, crackers, bread sticks (grissini) and poppadoms are good with cheese, dips and soups.

Jars and bottles

Curry pastes, which come in different strengths, are excellent for making quick vegetable, fish or meat curries, or for flavouring soups.

Passata (sieved tomatoes) is invaluable for making quick pasta sauces.

Mayonnaise can be used in salad dressings or for making dips. Reduced-fat versions are widely available.

Unsaturated oils such as sunflower, groundnut and olive are the healthy choice for cooking. Sesame oil is excellent for adding flavour to stir-fry dishes. Olive oil, the most versatile and tastiest of vegetable oils, is perfect for salad dressings, while walnut and hazelnut oils add a delicious nutty flavour.

Wine and cider vinegars are essential for salad dressings and for quick sweet and sour sauces. Balsamic vinegar has a rich flavour and dark colour from being aged in barrels for several years. Although expensive, it is used in small quantities.

Soy sauce and other Oriental sauces such as oyster, chilli and hoisin, and pastes such as miso and sesame, are good for flavouring quick-cook foods, as are mustards, Worcestershire sauce and Tabasco sauce.

Dried herbs and spices can add good flavour to a fast dish. Buy them in small quantities and use up within a few months. Jars of chopped garlic, lemongrass and ginger in sunflower oil are another great boon to the fast food cook.

Fresh produce out of the fridge

Bananas are best stored in a cool room. The skins go black in the fridge, although the flesh is not harmed.

Tomatoes are best kept at room temperature to develop their flavour; only refrigerate if they are very ripe and in danger of going mouldy.

Avocados do not ripen properly below 7°C (45°F), so only store in the fridge if ripe.

Potatoes should be kept above 4°C (39°F) so their starch content does not turn to sugar.

In the fridge

The fridge is the first port of call for most people looking for something to eat in a hurry. Instant snacks can be made from things like cheese and ham, but a varied choice of chilled and frozen foods means you have the makings of all kinds of quickly prepared, healthy meals for all the family.

The fridge is excellent for storing foods such as dairy products, along with fresh vegetables, fruit and eggs, all extremely versatile and ready to use at a moment's notice. The following is a handy checklist.

Semi-skimmed milk has all the nutrients of full-fat milk but less than half the fat. Used for white sauces and milk shakes, it dramatically reduces their fat content. Children under the age of 2 should not have low-fat foods, as they have high energy needs and require the fat and calories of full-fat milk.

Yogurt can be stirred into soups to garnish or thicken, and into hot spicy dishes to cool them. Add chopped mint and cucumber to yogurt to make a side dish to accompany hot spicy curries. Blend yogurt with fruit to make smoothies, or serve with desserts instead of cream and rich sauces.

Crème fraîche (half-fat, if you prefer) and single and soured cream are good lower-fat alternatives to double cream for sauces and desserts as well as savoury dishes.

Cheese, which provides the calcium needed for strong bones and teeth, is one of the most versatile ingredients to have in the

fridge. It goes well with crusty bread, eggs, salads, pasta, pulses and vegetables, and is useful for sprinkling or making sauces. The cheeses with a high fat content, such as mature Cheddar, Parmesan, Gruyère and Stilton, also have a strong flavour, so a little goes a long way. Lower-fat cheeses include fresh ricotta, smooth quark, creamy fromage frais, and curd and cottage cheeses, all of which are good in both sweet and savoury dishes.

Eggs can make a quick nutritious meal by themselves or they can be added to rice and grain dishes and salads. **Fruit** such as apples, apricots, grapes and berries can be used in sweet and savoury dishes, or eaten as vitamin-rich snacks.

Don't wash berries before refrigerating as this encourages mould. For the best flavour, bring all chilled fruit to room temperature before eating.

Bought prepared vegetables
are a time-saver for a fast cook. Those packed whole, such as mange-tout or baby corn, are excellent for stir-fries. Note, though, that packed cut-up vegetables and ready-washed salads lose their vitamin content more quickly than uncut vegetables and salad leaves.

Mayonnaise and most other sauces in jars need to be refrigerated after opening. Cans may rust in the fridge, so

transfer food from opened cans to other containers and cover.

Fresh stock, either home-made or in bought cartons, gives valuable flavour to rice dishes and quick soups and sauces.

Fridge know-how

Bought chilled food should be kept in the fridge, following the storage instructions on the pack. The 'best before' and 'use-by' dates apply only when a product is sealed – once opened, most foods should be refrigerated and used within 2–3 days. Don't overload the fridge and don't open the door more than necessary. Fridge temperature should be no higher than 5°C (41°F) – low temperatures slow the growth of any harmful bacteria that might be present.

In the freezer

The freezer is ideal for storing home-cooked foods. Batch cooking specifically to fill the freezer will save time later. Alternatively, make extra portions when preparing meals. Home-made stock can also be safely frozen – freeze it in small units for faster thawing. Bought frozen food will be marked with a 'use by' date and this applies to the length of

time you can safely keep it in the freezer before use.

Bread is better frozen than stored in the fridge (it goes dry and stale). If you slice it before freezing, you can remove individual slices that will thaw quickly or can be toasted from frozen. Pitta bread can be toasted from frozen, and part-baked breads can be baked from frozen. Storage times for bread vary according to the type of bread. Commercially baked or home-made brown and white bread will keep up to 6 months; flat breads 4 months; milk, fruit and malt breads 3 months. Breads with a crispy crust will keep for 2 weeks; after this the crust tends to break off as they thaw.

Breadcrumbs are good for toppings and can be used from frozen – the crumbs remain separate. Crumble day-old bread, or make large quantities in a blender, and freeze in polythene bags or plastic containers for up to 3 months. Croutons are another useful freezer item.

Frozen fruit and vegetables are nutritious and convenient – the vitamin content does not diminish during freezing. Fruit and vegetables thaw quickly or you can cook them from frozen.

Vegetable and fruit gluts can be frozen, although they may not be as nutritious as bought frozen produce, which is frozen within hours of picking. As a general rule, frozen vegetables can be stored for 10–12 months; fruit packed alone or as a purée will keep 6–8 months, packed in syrup or sugar 9–12 months.

Bought frozen yogurt, plain or with fruit, is an excellent stand-by for instant puddings, alone or with fresh fruit. Check the 'use by' date or store for up to 3 months.

Raw prawns and other shellfish can be cooked from frozen, as can fish fillets, to make a variety of quick meals. Store frozen fish according to the 'use by' date. If freezing fresh raw fish, store white fish for up to 3 months, oil-rich fish for up to 2 months. Most shellfish sold 'fresh' has been frozen and should not be frozen again.

Herbs can be frozen in stock or water in ice cube trays, or open-frozen and then packed into freezer containers or bags. Add the cubes to dishes as they are heating. Store for up to 6 months.

Pasta, plain or filled, can be cooked from frozen, needing only a simple sauce to transform it into a complete meal. It can be stored in the freezer for up to 1 month.

Grated cheese can be used from frozen in sauces or toppings. Store for up to 6 months.

Grated lemon, orange or lime zest, added frozen, will give instant flavour to many quick dishes. Open-freeze the zest on a tray and then pack into containers or bags. Store for up to 12 months.

Freezer know-how

Freezer temperature should be -18ºC (0ºF) or below. Most raw meat and poultry needs to be thawed before use; partially thawed poultry, for example, will not reach a high enough temperature when cooked to destroy any salmonella bacteria that might be present. Never refreeze thawed food unless you cook it in between, i.e. you can thaw raw chicken, cook it and then freeze the cooked dish, but you should never refreeze raw food that has been thawed, or cooked food that has been frozen, then thawed and reheated.

Good kitchen tools for fast food

The right kitchen tools, such as sharp knives, an electric mixer and a blender, can save time and effort when you are trying to prepare healthy fast food. Buy the best quality you can afford – with care, they will last a lifetime – and always keep tools in the same place, so you don't have to search the kitchen every time you want to use them.

Cutting tools

- Sharp knives make for fast work. They are also safer – accidents happen when trying to hack through food with a semi-blunt knife. A variety of knife sizes is essential: a small vegetable knife is excellent for chopping garlic or onions; a larger, heavier cook's knife is needed for pumpkin, swede and other hard vegetables; a filleting knife quickly removes fat from meat or skin from fish. A knife block will keep sharp blades covered (much safer than rooting around in a drawer) and means the knives are always visible and ready for action. Stainless steel blades do not rust and are dishwasher-proof; carbon steel knives are preferred by chefs because they can be sharpened (but then chefs have lots of help in the kitchen).
- Kitchen scissors are handy for snipping small amounts of herbs and for trimming and cutting cooked meats and bacon.

They are also good for trimming tough stalks off leafy vegetables or topping and tailing mange-tout, green beans, gooseberries and currants.

- A mezzaluna curved blade – with a handle at each end – will chop large quantities of herbs or nuts very quickly.

◀ Kitchen scissors will speed up preparation, such as topping and tailing fresh green beans

▼ The large curved blade of a mezzaluna chops bunches of herbs very fast

Basic knife selection

To cover the broad range of food preparation, a good basic knife selection should include (below, from left to right): a vegetable knife, a parer (or peeler), a filleting knife, a small cook's knife, a larger cook's knife, a carving knife and a bread knife.

Fast pans

● A wok is specially designed for stir-frying and can also be used for steaming – two quick and healthy cooking methods that use little or no fat.

● Cast-iron grill or griddle pans can be flat or ridged. They are heated on the hob before adding the food, which then cooks very quickly.

● Steamers can be made of metal with holes that allow the steam to reach the food or they can be Chinese-style bamboo ones with open slats. Whichever type you use, the food is placed in the steamer over boiling water and a lid is put on the top to prevent the steam from escaping.

● Pressure cooking, which steams food under pressure, retains more vitamins than boiling food. The pressurised container reduces cooking times dramatically – French onion soup takes 5 minutes cooking time, steamed fish and vegetables 4 minutes, and meat-based pasta sauces 10 minutes. Rice will cook in about 6 minutes (rice pudding in 10 minutes).

Grating and puréeing

● A hand-held grater is perfect for grating nutmeg, root ginger and cheese. A box grater with several sizes of grating blades is the most useful type.

● A mouli à légumes, or food mill, has stainless steel blades turned manually by a handle to make purées and mashed potato.

● Food processors make quick work of chopping, slicing, shredding and puréeing. Many have attachments such as meat mincers and juicers.

● Blenders are excellent for puréeing soups and sauces. Hand-held blenders can be used to purée small quantities directly in the pan or mixing bowl.

● Hand-held electric mixers quickly whisk egg whites or creamy mixtures.

● A pestle and mortar can be used for grinding spices or pulverising herbs, garlic and other foods. The mortar is a bowl-shaped container and the pestle is a rounded bat-like instrument that is pressed and rotated against the mortar to grind the food in it. A pestle and mortar can be made from stoneware, porcelain, marble or wood.

Speed techniques and time-savers

● A measuring jug cuts out the guesswork when you are trying to cook in a hurry. A heatproof glass jug can take hot liquids and be used to melt items in the microwave.

● A small whisk can quickly mix salad dressings. Put all the salad dressing ingredients in the bottom of the salad bowl to mix, rather than making the dressing separately. (Or make a larger quantity of vinaigrette dressing in a screw-top jar and keep in the fridge.) A small whisk will also ensure that sauces and custards do not go lumpy while cooking. A larger whisk makes quick work of whisking small amounts of egg white (when it is not worth getting out the electric mixer).

● Lemon squeezers have a ridged cone onto which a halved citrus fruit is pressed to make quick work of juicing it. Rolling the fruit on a worktop with the palm of your hand before squeezing it will yield more juice.

● A good-quality vegetable peeler with a swivel action blade will quickly peel vegetables, cutting away the minimum amount of skin.

● A garlic press is slightly quicker than a knife for crushing garlic cloves and it saves chopping boards or pestle and mortar being tainted with garlic. However, using a press gives a very strong garlic flavour. When really pushed for time, chopped garlic bottled in sunflower oil is a fast alternative.

● Kitchen scissors can be used to snip herbs or cooked meat or poultry directly over a salad – it is faster than chopping with a knife.

● A salad spinner will dry salad leaves in an instant.

● Make mess-free biscuit crumbs by crushing them in a strong polythene bag using a rolling pin.

● Preheat the oven before preparing ingredients unless using a fan oven. These cook food faster than conventional ovens and don't need preheating. (The recipe timings in this book are all for conventional ovens.)

● Heat the wok, grill or griddle when you start preparing a dish.

● Put the kettle on – the chances are you'll need boiling water, whether it's to steam or boil vegetables, or to cook pasta, rice or another grain. Small frozen items such as peas or beans can be thawed by placing them in a sieve and pouring boiling water (or even cold tap water) over them. It is also safe to do this with prawns, although the texture and flavour are better when prawns thaw slowly in the fridge.

◄ A garlic press squeezes the pulp directly from the unpeeled clove

► A hand-held blender is great for puréeing small quantities

▼ A small whisk can mix salad dressing directly in the bowl

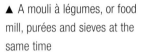

▲ A mouli à légumes, or food mill, purées and sieves at the same time

► A swivel-bladed vegetable peeler makes quick work of removing the skin

◄ Good pans for fast cooking are (from left to right) a steamer, a wok and a ridged cast-iron grill or griddle pan

► With a pressure cooker soup can be made in 5 minutes and a pasta sauce in 10, and more heat-sensitive vitamins are retained

In 15 Minutes or Less

Super snacks in almost no time at all

With the wealth of flavoursome breads available these days, you can make an endless variety of healthy lunches and snacks. Enjoy naan bread filled with a spicy mixture of lentils, vegetables and yogurt, or Mediterranean bruschettas with Parma ham, tomato and pesto. Or fill crusty mini baguettes with smoked turkey and salad. For a sweet treat, try malted fruit bread topped with soft cheese, strawberry and banana, or caramelised apple and fresh blackberries on toasted brioche. And for a delicious drink any time of day, whizz up a fruit smoothie.

Tomato and ham bruschettas

Capture the flavour of the Mediterranean with these bite-sized toasts topped with pesto sauce, thinly sliced Parma ham and tomatoes, a combination popular all along the Med in France and Italy. This recipe is an excellent way to make the most of leftover French bread, which becomes dry after just 1 day.

Serves 4

1 thin baguette, about 170 g (6 oz)

2 tbsp pesto sauce

85 g (3 oz) Parma ham, sliced wafer-thin and trimmed of all fat

3 vine-ripened tomatoes, about 85 g (3 oz) each, sliced

1 tbsp extra virgin olive oil

salt and pepper

rocket leaves to garnish

Preparation and cooking time: about 15 minutes

1 Preheat the grill to high. Slice the baguette into 12 equal slices. Place the slices on the rack in the grill pan and grill until toasted on the top side.

2 Turn the toasts over and spread with the pesto sauce. Top each with the Parma ham, cut and folded to fit on the bread. Divide the tomato slices among the toasts, then drizzle with the olive oil. Season to taste with salt and pepper.

3 Return the bruschettas to the grill and cook for 1–2 minutes or until the tomato slices begin to soften and char at the edges. Garnish each bruschetta with a few rocket leaves and serve hot or at room temperature.

Some more ideas

• For feta and tomato bruschettas, replace the Parma ham with 100 g (3½ oz) crumbled feta cheese, and use ciabatta instead of a baguette. Toast the slices of bread on one side, turn them over and brush with 2 tbsp extra virgin olive oil instead of the pesto sauce. Divide the feta cheese among the toasts and season with freshly ground black pepper (feta is salty, so you don't need to add salt). Grill until the cheese melts and bubbles. Garnish with fresh basil sprigs instead of rocket.

• Replace the pesto sauce with tapenade, a full-flavoured black olive spread popular in the Mediterranean. You only need ½ tsp for each bruschetta.

• Leftover grilled red, yellow or orange peppers, or grilled peppers in jars, are ideal to add to the bruschettas. Alternatively, if you have time, place fresh peppers under a preheated grill and grill until they are blistered and blackened all over. Put them in a polythene bag and leave until cool enough to handle, then peel off the skins and cut the flesh into slices.

Plus points

• Parma ham, the most famous of the Italian salted, air-dried prosciuttos, is a good lean alternative to bacon rashers, as long as you trim off all the fat.

• Raw tomatoes are an excellent source of vitamin C and a significant source of vitamin A from beta-carotene.

• Bread is an important part of a healthy diet as it is a starchy (complex) carbohydrate, and contributes vitamins and minerals.

Each serving provides

kcal 115, **protein** 6 g, **fat** 4 g (of which saturated fat 1 g), **carbohydrate** 12 g (of which sugars 1 g), **fibre** 0.5 g

✓ C

Naan bread with lentil caviar

Yogurt spiced with garlic and mint, then mixed with raw vegetables and high-protein lentils, is delicious spooned onto warmed naan bread. A few coriander and mint leaves on top add a touch of freshness, and a dab of chutney or lime pickle on the side gives texture and extra flavour.

Serves 4

Lentil 'caviar'

340 g (12 oz) plain low-fat yogurt

2 garlic cloves, chopped

1 can green lentils, about 300 g, drained

½ cucumber, finely chopped

½ green pepper, seeded and cut into fine dice

1 ripe tomato, finely chopped

1 tbsp chopped fresh mint

¼ tsp ground cumin, or to taste

large pinch of curry powder

juice of ½ lemon

2 tbsp extra virgin olive oil

salt and cayenne pepper

To serve

4 individual plain naans, cut into wedges

leaves from 3–4 sprigs of fresh mint

3 tbsp fresh coriander leaves

few rocket leaves

2 carrots, grated

2 tbsp chutney of choice or lime pickle

Preparation time: 15 minutes

Each serving provides ⓥ

kcal 420, **protein** 17 g, **fat** 14 g (of which saturated fat 1 g), **carbohydrate** 60 g (of which sugars 20 g), **fibre** 6 g

✓✓✓	A, C
✓✓	B₁, B₂, B₆, folate, calcium, copper, iron, selenium, zinc
✓	E, B₁₂, potassium

1 Preheat the grill. Mix together all the ingredients for the lentil 'caviar' and season with salt and cayenne pepper to taste.

2 Sprinkle the naans with water, then place under the grill and toast for 1 minute on each side. Transfer them to individual plates.

3 Spoon the lentil 'caviar' over the warm breads, dividing it equally among them. Sprinkle with the fresh mint, coriander and rocket leaves and the grated carrots. Serve at once, with the chutney or lime pickle on the side.

Some more ideas

• You can use garlic naan or peshwari naan, although these have a higher fat and calorie content than plain naan.

• Keep some pre-cooked lentils in your freezer; that way, even if plain cooked lentils in a can are not readily available, you can still make this tasty snack. Lentils thaw easily, especially in a microwave, or heated on the hob, or simply left out at room temperature.

• Use 100 g (3½ oz) shredded red cabbage instead of the grated carrot.

• For chickpea and spinach naans, make the 'caviar' with 1 can chickpeas, about 400 g, drained, instead of lentils, and omit the cucumber, green pepper and tomato. Cook 225 g (8 oz) spinach leaves, either by steaming or boiling for 3 minutes, or microwave in the cellophane bag if using ready-prepared spinach. Squeeze dry, then chop coarsely. Divide the spinach among the naans, top with spoonfuls of the chickpea 'caviar' and garnish with the mint, coriander and rocket. Serve with wedges of lemon to squeeze over the top.

• Fill pitta breads with the lentil or chickpea 'caviar'. Warm 4 pitta breads in a toaster or under the grill until they puff up, then slash open to form a pocket. Fill each one with 'caviar' and add a handful of grated carrot or cabbage and a dab of chutney or lime pickle.

Plus points

• Like all beans and pulses, lentils are a good source of soluble fibre – the type that can help to reduce high blood cholesterol levels. Unlike other beans, lentils don't need to be soaked overnight, but they do take about 20 minutes to cook, so when time is short canned lentils are a good alternative. The canning process does not reduce the fibre content.

• Yogurt is a useful source of calcium, phosphorus and vitamins B₂ and B₁₂.

• The large amount of beta-carotene and other carotenoids in carrots makes them an excellent source of vitamin A. Carrots also contain some vitamin C and niacin and a small amount of vitamin E.

Pasta with two-cheese sauce

After a busy day, this is one of the quickest options for a nutritious family meal – the cheese mixture is prepared in the time it takes the pasta and peas to cook. When you add the hot pasta to the Parmesan and ricotta, the heat melts them, producing an instant creamy sauce. Green and purple basil makes a colourful garnish.

Serves 4

400 g (14 oz) fusilli (spirals) or other pasta
   shapes
225 g (8 oz) frozen peas
45 g (1½ oz) Parmesan cheese, freshly grated
2 tbsp extra virgin olive oil
150 g (5½ oz) ricotta cheese
finely torn fresh basil or oregano
salt and pepper

Preparation and cooking time: 15 minutes

Each serving provides   Ⓥ
kcal 535, **protein** 22 g, **fat** 15 g (of which saturated fat 6 g), **carbohydrate** 81 g (of which sugars 4 g), **fibre** 6 g

✓✓	calcium, coppor, iron, zinc
✓	A, B$_1$, B$_{12}$, folate, niacin, selenium

1 Cook the pasta in boiling water for 7 minutes. Add the peas, return the water to the boil and continue cooking for 3–5 minutes, or according to the pasta packet instructions, until the pasta is al dente and the peas are cooked.

2 Meanwhile, put the Parmesan cheese into a large serving bowl, add the olive oil and beat until a thick paste forms. Add the ricotta cheese and beat until well blended. Season with salt and pepper to taste.

3 Drain the pasta, reserving about 6 tbsp of the cooking water. Immediately add the hot pasta to the cheese mixture and stir until the pasta is well coated. Add the reserved cooking water to thin the sauce.

4 Adjust the seasoning, if necessary, and sprinkle generously with fresh basil or oregano. Serve at once.

Some more ideas
● All kinds of vegetables can be used in this dish. If fresh, chop or slice them small enough so that they cook in the time it takes to cook the pasta. Try broccoli florets, grated carrots, green beans or sweetcorn kernels.
● Stir in grated raw courgettes or carrots at the end of step 3. Raw vegetables are particularly high in fibre and vitamins.
● Sun-dried tomatoes, well drained and cut into thin strips, can be added to the cheese sauce.

● For a Mediterranean-style dish of pasta and broad beans with a quick cheese sauce, replace the peas with frozen or fresh broad beans. Mash 100 g (3½ oz) drained feta cheese, then beat in 50 g (1¾ oz) soft goat's cheese to make a thick paste. Stir in a little of the pasta cooking water to thin the sauce, if necessary, and season with salt, pepper and a little freshly grated lemon zest. Stir in finely chopped fresh dill just before serving.

Plus points
● Parmesan cheese, traditionally served with so many pasta dishes, is very high in fat. Here only a small amount is used for its distinctive flavour, and it is combined with ricotta cheese which is relatively low in fat – ricotta contains 11 g fat per 100 g (3½ oz), while the same weight of full-fat soft cheese has 47 g fat
● Peas are a good source of fibre and they supply vitamin C, folate, iron and zinc. Peas also contribute B vitamins, in particular B$_1$, and their protein content is high for a vegetable that also provides a useful amount of folate.

in 15 minutes or less

Dolcelatte and pear sandwiches

Slices of fresh juicy pear, tasty blue cheese and pecan nuts on lightly toasted slices of bread make a lovely flavour combination in these simple open sandwiches. Cut generous slices of bread for a truly delicious and carbohydrate-rich snack. Cherry tomatoes are the perfect accompaniment.

Serves 4

2 ripe pears, preferably red-skinned

lemon juice

200 g (7 oz) wedge of Dolcelatte cheese

30 g (1 oz) pecan nuts

8 large slices of baguette, about 2 cm (¾ in) thick

4 tbsp mango chutney

30 g (1 oz) watercress sprigs

30 g (1 oz) rocket

pepper

cherry tomatoes to serve

Preparation time: about 15 minutes

1 Preheat the grill. Core and quarter or slice the pears, then toss with a squeeze of lemon juice to prevent the pears from discolouring. Cut the cheese down the length of the wedge to make 8 thin, triangular slices.

2 Lightly toast the pecan nuts under the grill, watching carefully to make sure they don't burn, then roughly chop them. Set aside. Spread out the bread slices on the grill pan and toast lightly on both sides.

3 Spread the mango chutney on the toasted bread and top with the watercress and rocket. Arrange a slice of cheese and a quarter of the pears on each piece of toast and scatter over the pecan nuts. Season with pepper. Serve at once, with halved cherry tomatoes.

Some more ideas

● Use Granary or wholemeal bread instead of baguette to increase fibre content.

● Substitute thin slices of Stilton cheese for the Dolcelatte, and replace the pecan nuts with walnuts.

● Replace the pears with 2 star fruit, cut into thin slices.

● To make Cheddar, date and apple open sandwiches, use 8 slices of walnut bread, toasting it, if liked. Top each slice with a small leaf of cos lettuce and a little watercress. Cover with thin slices of Cheddar cheese and apple slices, then scatter over 4 stoned and chopped fresh dates, preferably Medjool from California which are deliciously moist.

Plus points

● Cheese is a good source of protein, calcium, phosphorus and the vitamins B_2 and B_{12}. Although Dolcelatte is high in fat, its strong flavour means a little goes a long way.

● Slicing the bread thickly will increase the ratio of starchy carbohydrate to fat, thus helping to make this a healthy balanced dish.

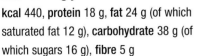

Each serving provides

kcal 440, **protein** 18 g, **fat** 24 g (of which saturated fat 12 g), **carbohydrate** 38 g (of which sugars 16 g), **fibre** 5 g

✓✓ A, B_1, B_2, B_{12}, C, folate, calcium, copper, iron, selenium, zinc

✓ B_6, niacin

Smoked turkey baguettines

Mini baguettes, with their crusty exteriors and soft interiors, are the ideal breads for filling with all kinds of nutritious ingredients to make a quick snack. Here a combination of crisp and chewy vegetables is mixed with delicious smoked turkey from the delicatessen counter for a healthy and substantial sandwich.

Serves 4

4 baguettines, about 600 g (1 lb 5 oz) in total

2 heads of chicory, about 250 g (8½ oz) in total

2 cartons mustard and cress

350 g (12½ oz) skinned and boned smoked turkey breast, thinly sliced

1 large yellow pepper, seeded and thinly sliced

2 celery sticks, cut diagonally into 4 cm (1½ in) pieces

Chive dressing

3 tbsp extra virgin olive oil

1 tbsp lemon juice

1 tsp Dijon mustard

1 tbsp snipped fresh chives

salt and pepper

Preparation time: 15 minutes

1 Using a sharp bread knife, split the baguettines open along the top. Cut the chicory into diagonal slices about 1 cm (½ in) thick. Snip the mustard and cress using kitchen scissors.

2 To make the dressing, mix together all the ingredients and season with salt and pepper to taste.

3 To assemble the rolls, arrange the slices of chicory and mustard and cress in the base of each slit-open baguettine, then add the slices of turkey. Arrange the pepper and celery slices on top of the turkey. Drizzle the dressing over the filling. Serve within 1 hour.

Some more ideas

● Split the baguettines in half horizontally. Arrange the filling on the bottom half, then place the bread lid on top. Insert 2 or 3 cocktail sticks into the baguettines to hold them together, if wished.

● For salmon baguettines, replace the turkey with 2 cans of salmon, about 180 g each. Drain the salmon and flake the flesh, then mix with 2 spring onions, finely chopped. Make up the dressing using lime juice in place of the lemon juice. Combine the dressing with the salmon, then assemble the baguettines as in the main recipe, using a red pepper rather than yellow.

Plus points

● If you have the time, it's always better to make your own dressing rather than using a shop-bought one. Not only will it taste better, but you can control the amount and type of oil you use. Also, being fresh and flavoured with fresh herbs, mustard, black pepper and so on, the dressing has no need for flavour enhancers or preservatives.

● Turkey is an excellent source of lean, low-fat protein as well as vitamin B_{12}, niacin and zinc.

● The ancient Egyptians, Greeks and Romans all used chicory as a medicinal remedy as well as a food – it was believed to help stimulate digestive fluids and strengthen the liver. Naturopaths often recommend using chicory leaves as a poultice for swollen joints. They suggest you steam or microwave the leaves and place them on the affected area for 15 minutes.

Each serving provides

kcal 580, **protein** 34 g, **fat** 14 g (of which saturated fat 2 g), **carbohydrate** 85 g (of which sugars 6 g), **fibre** 4 g

✓✓✓	B_6, B_{12}, C, selenium
✓✓	B_1, niacin, calcium, zinc
✓	B_2, folate, copper, iron, potassium

in 15 minutes or less

34

Ham and celeriac pittas

This refreshing salad sandwich is packed with a mixture of crunchy vegetables, smoked ham, dried fruit and green olives that gives lovely contrasting flavours and textures. The tangy mustard dressing is based on Greek-style yogurt and mayonnaise. Add a piece of fresh fruit and you have a really healthy lunch.

Serves 6

125 g (4½ oz) piece celeriac

2 carrots, about 150 g (5½ oz) in total

170 g (6 oz) thickly sliced lean smoked ham, cut into 1 cm (½ in) dice

1 small red onion, thinly sliced

8 stoned green olives, pimiento-stuffed if wished, halved

50 g (1¾ oz) currants

2 tbsp chopped parsley

6 garlic pitta breads

1 heart of romaine or cos lettuce, finely shredded

parsley to garnish

Mustard dressing

3 tbsp Greek-style yogurt

½ tsp wholegrain mustard

2 tbsp mayonnaise

Preparation time: 15 minutes

1 Preheat the grill to high. Mix together all the dressing ingredients in a medium-sized bowl.

2 Peel and coarsely grate the celeriac and carrots. Add to the bowl of dressing and mix well. Add the ham, onion, olives, currants and chopped parsley and mix everything together.

3 Warm the pitta breads under the grill for about 1 minute on each side. Cut each one across in half to make 2 pockets of bread. Divide the lettuce among the pitta pockets, then add the ham and celeriac salad. Garnish with parsley and serve.

Some more ideas

• To reduce the total fat content you can use 0%-fat Greek-style yogurt and reduced-fat mayonnaise. The dressing will still be deliciously creamy.

• For chicken, apple and celery pittas, cut 375 g (13 oz) cooked skinless boneless chicken breasts (fillets) into thin slices. Toss 1 green apple, diced, 3 celery sticks, thinly sliced, and 4 spring onions, sliced, with the mustard dressing. Fold in the chicken. Put some shredded lettuce and a small handful of rocket or watercress leaves into each pitta pocket, then add the chicken salad.

• Make ham and celeriac wraps by rolling the shredded lettuce and ham mixture in 4 large flour tortillas. The chicken filling is also delicious in wraps.

Plus points

• Celeriac is related to celery and, like celery, it provides potassium. When eaten raw as in these sandwiches, it also offers vitamin C.

• Currants provide a useful amount of fibre and some magnesium, which is important for healthy bones, the release of energy from food, and nerve and muscle function.

Each serving provides

kcal 320, **protein** 13 g, **fat** 6 g (of which saturated fat 1 g), **carbohydrate** 54 g (of which sugars 11 g), **fibre** 3 g

✓✓✓	A
✓✓	B₁
✓	B₆, C, folate, calcium, copper, iron

Smoked mackerel stacks

These triple-decker sandwiches are best made with bread that is firm enough to slice thinly but is not heavy. Rye bread is tasty with mackerel – look for one made with wheat and rye flour – or use wholemeal or Granary bread. Spreading the fish mixture on both sides of the middle slice of bread holds the sandwich together.

Serves 4

200 g (7 oz) skinless smoked mackerel fillet

100 g (3½ oz) quark

1 tsp grated fresh horseradish

12 thin slices rye bread

4 tomatoes, thinly sliced

½ cucumber, thinly sliced

8 tbsp snipped mustard and cress, plus extra mustard and cress to garnish

Preparation time: 15 minutes

1 Remove any bones from the mackerel fillet. Chop the flesh coarsely, then mash with the quark and horseradish until well blended to a paste.

2 Spread the slices of bread out on a clean work surface, arranging them in 4 rows of 3 slices each. Reserve one-quarter of the mackerel paste, then divide the remainder evenly among the slices of bread, spreading it smoothly.

3 Using half of the tomato and cucumber slices, arrange them on 4 of the mackerel-spread bread slices. Sprinkle over half of the mustard and cress. Top each with a second piece of bread, mackerel-side down. Spread the rest of the mackerel mixture on the top side of these slices of bread. Arrange the remaining tomato and cucumber slices on top and sprinkle over the rest of the mustard and cress. Place the last slices of bread on top, mackerel side down, and press together gently.

4 Cut the sandwich stacks into 3 or 4 pieces, depending on the shape of the bread, and pierce each piece with a cocktail stick to secure the stacked layers. Garnish each stack with extra mustard and cress and serve.

Some more ideas

● For chillied prawn and sun-dried tomato stacks, make the filling with 225 g (8 oz) cooked peeled tiger prawns, chopped, 200 g (7 oz) quark, 2 tbsp finely chopped sun-dried tomatoes and ½ tsp chilli purée. Use slices of olive bread, with tomato slices and mustard and cress as in the main recipe.

● Substitute finely chopped rocket for the mustard and cress.

● If quark is hard to find, you can use reduced-fat soft cheese or fromage frais instead.

Plus points

● Smoked mackerel is ideal for quick, tasty and nutritious meals, as it requires very little preparation but has a lot to offer nutritionally. In common with other oily fish, such as salmon, herring and sardines, mackerel is rich in omega-3 fatty acids, a type of polyunsaturated fat thought to help protect against coronary heart disease and strokes by making blood less sticky and less likely to clot. A diet rich in omega-3 fatty acids may also be helpful in preventing and treating arthritis.

● Quark, a yogurt cheese that is low In fat and sodium, is a particularly healthy option for a creamy sandwich filling.

Each serving provides

kcal 400, **protein** 21 g, **fat** 17 g (of which saturated fat 3 g), **carbohydrate** 44 g (of which sugars 5 g), **fibre** 5 g

✓✓✓	B$_6$, B$_{12}$, C
✓✓	B$_1$, B$_2$, folate, niacin, iron
✓	A, E, selenium, zinc

in 15 minutes or less

Fruit bread slices

If you're bored with cereal for breakfast, try this vitamin-packed fruity alternative. Thick slices of malt bread, toasted and spread with orange-flavoured soft cheese, are topped with sliced strawberries and bananas. Cut the loaf lengthways and allow 2 slices per portion, or cut crossways for 3–4 slices each.

Serves 4

115 g (4 oz) reduced-fat soft cheese

grated zest and juice of 1 small orange

2 bananas

225 g (8 oz) strawberries, sliced

1 large fruited malted loaf, about 250 g (8½ oz), sliced (see above)

soft brown or demerara sugar for sprinkling (optional)

Preparation time: 15 minutes

1 Preheat the grill to high. Mix the soft cheese with half of the orange zest. Slice the bananas and toss in the orange juice together with the sliced strawberries.

2 Toast the bread under the hot grill for 2 minutes on each side or until lightly browned. Spread the toasted bread with the cheese and arrange the banana and strawberry slices on top. Sprinkle each slice with a pinch of brown or demerara sugar, if liked, and with the rest of the orange zest. Serve immediately.

Some more ideas

• The cheese and fruit topping can also be spread over toasted cinnamon and raisin bread, Granary bread or muesli bread. As these breads tend to be larger, increase the quantity of soft cheese to 170 g (6 oz) and add a little more orange zest.

• For garlicky ham and tomato slices, toast 4 slices of malted oat or pumpkin bread and spread with 85 g (3 oz) low-fat garlic and herb soft cheese. Top with 100 g (3½ oz) quartered cherry tomatoes and 100 g (3½ oz) ham in wafer-thin slices. Another delicious alternative is to use chopped papaya in place of the tomatoes.

• For a naturally sweet, completely fat-free date and orange spread, cook 250 g (8½ oz) stoned dates in 450 ml (15 fl oz) orange juice, or a mixture of orange juice and water, in a covered saucepan for 10 minutes or until soft. Leave to cool, then purée in a food processor or blender until smooth, or beat with a fork for a rougher consistency. Spread a little of the purée over toasted Irish sultana soda bread, cinnamon and raisin bread, or muesli bread, and top with sliced bananas. Leftover spread can be stored in a covered container in the fridge for up to 1 week. This makes 450 ml (15 fl oz).

Plus points

• A high-fibre cereal is definitely the healthy choice first thing in the morning, but once in a while it's nice to have something different, and these fruit bread slices are a good alternative. They provide a healthy balance of nutrients – fibre and potassium from the bananas, vitamin C from the strawberries and orange juice, calcium and vitamins B_2 and B_{12} from the cheese, and starchy carbohydrate from the bread.

• More and more supermarkets are now selling a range of gourmet breads speckled with interesting and tasty grains, nuts and seeds. They not only taste good, but are a great way to add fibre to your family's diet without them realising it.

Each serving provides Ⓥ

kcal 260, protein 8 g, fat 4 g (of which saturated fat 3 g), carbohydrate 45 g (of which sugars 28 g), fibre 1 g

✓✓✓	C
✓✓	B_1, B_6
✓	B_{12}, niacin, calcium, iron

Apple and blackberry brioches

An irresistible way to start the day – toasted slices of brioche topped with caramelised apple rings and fresh blackberries, with a subtle cinnamon flavour. Made with butter and eggs, brioche has a slightly higher fat content than white bread, but it is still a deliciously healthy source of starchy carbohydrate.

Serves 4

25 g (scant 1 oz) butter

4 apples

½ tsp ground cinnamon

4 individual brioches

200 g (7 oz) fresh blackberries

4 tsp demerara sugar

Preparation and cooking time: 15 minutes

1 Preheat the grill. Line the grill pan with foil, put the butter on top and set it under the grill to melt. Meanwhile, core the apples and slice each one into 6 rings, discarding the outer edge pieces. Dip the apple rings in the melted butter to coat both sides, then lay them out in a single layer on the foil and sprinkle with the cinnamon.

2 Grill the apple rings for about 4 minutes or until they are starting to brown, turning them over once. Remove the apples on their foil from the grill pan and set aside.

3 Slice each brioche horizontally into 3 and spread out the slices in the grill pan. Toast lightly on both sides. Place 2 apple rings on top of each toasted brioche slice, add a few blackberries and sprinkle with the sugar. Put back under the grill and warm the berries for 2–3 minutes, then serve.

Some more ideas

• For a higher energy breakfast, make banana and raspberry toasts. Toast 4 slices of white or wholemeal bread or Jewish challah bread. Arrange 2 large bananas, sliced, and 100 g (3½ oz) raspberries on top, covering the toast to the edges. Top with 25 g (scant 1 oz) butter, cut in little pieces, and sprinkle each with 1 tsp light soft brown sugar. Grill until starting to brown and caramelise.

• Try orange and strawberry-topped muffins. Toast 4 split wholemeal muffins, then top with 2 oranges, divided into segments, and halved strawberries. Sprinkle each muffin with 2 tsp demerara sugar. Grill until the fruit sizzles.

• Drop scones or scotch pancakes can be topped with sliced kiwi fruit and orange, or strawberries and grapes.

Plus points

• Apples contribute pectin, a soluble fibre that helps to reduce the highs and lows in blood sugar levels and also helps to lower blood cholesterol. This makes apples a great start to the day.

• Blackberries are a useful source of the antioxidant vitamin E, which can help to protect against heart disease and keep the skin in good condition. They are also a good source of vitamin C and bioflavonoid compounds.

• A recent study of over 2500 middle-aged men living in the Caerphilly area found that those who ate 5 or more apples per week had stronger lungs than those men who ate no apples. Apples contain high levels of a flavonoid called quercetin (also found in onions, tea and red wine), which is thought to have a potent antioxidant effect and may help to protect the lungs from damage.

Each serving provides Ⓥ

kcal 280, **protein** 5 g, **fat** 10 g (of which saturated fat 6 g), **carbohydrate** 44 g (of which sugars 31 g), **fibre** 4 g

✓✓	C, E
✓	B₆

Banana and apricot smoothie

Take a new look at the milkshake – it's been reinvented. Nowadays it is fresher and lighter, made with lots of fruit and yogurt, fruit juice or milk for a drink that's bursting with vitamins and minerals. It's ideal when you have little time for breakfast, and is also great as a mid-morning drink or an after-school snack.

Serves 4

2 large bananas, about 300 g (10½ oz) in total, thickly sliced

1 can apricot halves in natural juice, about 400 g

200 g (7 oz) plain low-fat bio yogurt

4 tsp chopped fresh mint

1 tbsp clear honey

300 ml (10 fl oz) bought 'freshly squeezed' orange juice

sprigs of fresh mint to decorate

Preparation time: 10 minutes

1 Put the bananas, apricots and their juice, yogurt, mint and honey into a food processor or blender and blend to a smooth purée, scraping down the sides of the container once or twice. Add the orange juice and blend briefly until mixed.

2 Pour the smoothie into tall glasses and decorate with sprigs of mint. Serve immediately.

Some more ideas

• For a strawberry and banana smoothie, instead of apricots use 225 g (8 oz) strawberries. Reserve 4 strawberries and blend the remainder with the bananas and yogurt (there is no need to add honey or mint). Mix in apple juice in place of the orange juice. Stir in the grated zest and juice of 1 lime and the seeds from 2 halved passion fruit. Pour into glasses and decorate each one with a reserved strawberry skewered on a cocktail stick and placed across the top of the glass. This makes 900 ml (1½ pints) to serve 3–4.

• For a peach and cinnamon smoothie, blend 1 can peaches in natural juice, about 400 g, with 1 tbsp muscovado sugar, ¼ tsp ground cinnamon and the bananas and yogurt. Add semi-skimmed milk in place of the orange juice. Sprinkle each glass with a little extra cinnamon. This makes 1 litre (1¾ pints) to serve 4.

• For a pineapple and peach smoothie, blend 1 can of pineapple rings in natural juice, about 225 g, with 200 g (7 oz) low-fat peach and pineapple yogurt and 150 ml (5 fl oz) orange juice until the fruit is finely chopped. This makes 600 ml (1 pint) to serve 2–3.

• For spiced banana smoothie, omit the canned apricots and mint, and use semi-skimmed milk instead of the orange juice. Flavour with a generous pinch of grated nutmeg and a pinch each of ground ginger and cardamom. Pour into glasses and decorate with thinly sliced pistachio nuts. This makes 600 ml (1 pint) to serve 2–3.

Plus points

• Many children are reluctant to eat fruit as they think that it takes too much effort. Transforming it into a drink is the ideal way to get round this, and fun too if the smoothie is served with wide spiral straws.

• Bananas are a good source of potassium, which is vital for muscle and nerve function and to help regulate blood pressure. They are also naturally sweet.

• These drinks are completely additive free, unlike their shop-bought counterparts.

Each serving provides

Ⓥ

kcal 180, **protein** 4 g, **fat** 1 g (of which saturated fat 0.5 g), **carbohydrate** 40 g (of which sugars 38 g), **fibre** 2 g

✓✓✓	C
✓✓	B_6
✓	B_1, B_2, folate, calcium, potassium

For Maximum Vitality

Raw-energy, vitamin-rich fast foods

Eating fruit and vegetables raw is the best way to maximise their health-giving benefits, and it is also the fastest way to enjoy them. In sweet or savoury salads, Mexican-style salsas, crudités or fruit kebabs, they combine with quick-cooking foods like lean bacon, boneless duck breasts, tiger prawns and fresh tuna to produce nutritious meals in a matter of minutes. They also add fresh colour and flavour to useful storecupboard ingredients such as canned pulses, and to air-cured beef and ham from the delicatessen counter.

Bacon and broad bean salad

This delicious warm salad is packed with strong flavours and makes a fabulous supper or lunch served with chunks of crusty bread or a side dish of new potatoes. Use a mild smoked bacon, such as a maple cure, as it is slightly less salty than some of the other cures.

Serves 4

1 tbsp sunflower oil

200 g (7 oz) lean smoked back bacon, rinded and snipped into large pieces

1 large red pepper, seeded and cut into strips

2 red onions, cut into wedges

2 slices of bread

400 g (14 oz) frozen broad beans, thawed

2 small firm heads of radicchio, cut into wedges

chopped fresh flat-leaf parsley to garnish (optional)

Devilled dressing

4 tbsp mayonnaise

2 tsp Worcestershire sauce

1 tbsp Dijon mustard

generous pinch of caster sugar

3–4 tbsp milk

salt and pepper

Preparation and cooking time: 30 minutes

Each serving provides

kcal 350, **protein** 19 g, **fat** 20 g (of which saturated fat 4 g), **carbohydrate** 24 g (of which sugars 9 g), **fibre** 8 g

✓✓✓	C, folate
✓✓	A, B$_1$, B$_2$, B$_6$, zinc
✓	copper, iron

1 Preheat the grill if not using a toaster for the bread. Make the dressing by mixing together the mayonnaise, Worcestershire sauce, Dijon mustard and sugar. Add enough milk to make a drizzling consistency. Season with salt and pepper to taste, and set aside.

2 Heat the sunflower oil in a large saucepan. Add the bacon, red pepper and onions, and fry over a high heat for 4 minutes, stirring, until the onions have softened.

3 Meanwhile, toast the bread in a toaster or under the grill. Cut it into cubes. Set aside.

4 Stir the broad beans into the bacon mixture and add 1 tbsp water. Heat until sizzling, then cover the pan and leave to cook for 4 minutes.

5 Arrange the wedges of radicchio on top of the bean and bacon mixture. Cover again and cook for 3 minutes or until the radicchio has wilted, but still holds its shape.

6 Spoon the salad into shallow bowls and drizzle over the dressing. Scatter the toasted bread cubes over the top, sprinkle with chopped flat-leaf parsley and serve.

Some more ideas

● If radicchio is unavailable, you can use 300 g (10½ oz) chicory or 2 crisp Little Gem lettuces.

● For a wilted chicory and bacon salad, make an orange and honey dressing by mixing the grated zest of ½ orange with 4 tbsp orange juice, 1 tbsp each lemon juice and honey, 2 tbsp extra virgin olive oil and 1 tsp balsamic vinegar. Season to taste. Cut the peel and pith from 2 oranges and slice between the membrane to release the segments. Cook the bacon, pepper and onion as in the main recipe, then add 340 g (12 oz) frozen peas instead of the broad beans. Cook for 4 minutes. Add 2 heads of chicory, cut into wedges, and cook for 2 more minutes. Toss with the orange segments, dressing and 45 g (1½ oz) watercress. Scatter over 45 g (1½ oz) toasted pecan nuts and serve warm.

Plus point

● Broad beans are a good source of soluble fibre, and one serving of this dish provides around one-third of the recommended daily amount. Broad beans also offer useful amounts of phosphorus, copper and the flavonoid quercetin, which can help to protect against heart disease.

for maximum vitality

Tiger prawns with pepper salsa

A salsa is a Mexican-style vegetable or fruit sauce with a fresh zingy flavour. A tomato, pepper and chilli salsa makes a wonderful accompaniment for grilled prawn kebabs, here served with sweet melon and crusty bread.

Serves 4

32 large raw tiger prawns, peeled but tails left on

1 Charentais melon, seeded and cut into cubes

Marinade

2 tbsp lime juice

1 tsp bottled chopped garlic in oil, drained

1 tsp bottled chopped root ginger in oil, drained

Salsa

6 vine-ripened tomatoes, chopped

1 small red onion, finely chopped

1 red pepper, seeded and chopped

1 tsp bottled chopped garlic in oil, drained

1 fresh green chilli, seeded and finely chopped

2 tbsp lime juice

2 tbsp chopped fresh coriander

salt and pepper

shredded spring onions to garnish

Preparation and cooking time: 30 minutes

Each serving provides

kcal 150, **protein** 24 g, **fat** 1.5 g (of which saturated fat 0.5 g), **carbohydrate** 11 g (of which sugars 10 g), **fibre** 3 g

✓✓✓	A, B$_{12}$, C
✓✓	B$_6$, iron
✓	folate, niacin, potassium, selenium, zinc

1 Preheat the grill. Soak 8 bamboo skewers in cold water (this will prevent them from burning under the grill). Combine all of the ingredients for the marinade in a shallow dish. Add the prawns and stir to coat them with the marinade. Cover and chill while preparing the salsa.

2 Mix together all the salsa ingredients and season with salt and pepper to taste. Pile into a serving bowl. Thread the cubes of melon onto 8 unsoaked wooden skewers and place on a serving dish. Set aside.

3 Thread 4 prawns onto each of the soaked skewers, piercing them through both ends (this will help to keep them flat). Place under the grill and cook for 3–4 minutes or until they are pink, turning them once. Do not overcook or they will become tough.

4 Garnish the salsa with the shredded spring onions. Place the prawn kebabs on the serving dish with the melon and serve immediately, with the salsa alongside.

Some more ideas

● Make grilled chicken kebabs and serve with a fresh citrus salsa. Cut 550 g (1¼ lb) skinless boneless chicken breasts (fillets) into cubes and marinate as described in the main recipe. Grill the chicken on skewers for 10 minutes or until tender and cooked through. For the salsa, chop the flesh from 1 pink grapefruit and 1 orange and 1 crisp juicy apple (such as Jonagold), and mix with 2 chopped spring onions, 1 finely chopped fresh green chilli and 1 tbsp chopped fresh mint.

● Cubes of fresh pineapple can be speared onto skewers to accompany the prawn or chicken kebabs in place of melon.

Plus points

● The raw fruit and vegetables in the salsa are packed with vitamins. The tomatoes and red peppers are excellent sources of the antioxidants beta-carotene and vitamin C. Red peppers, in particular, are an excellent source of vitamin C. Weight for weight, they provide over twice as much vitamin C as oranges.

● Prawns are a high-protein, low-fat food.

Swedish rollmop, beetroot and orange salad

Jars of rollmops (filleted pickled herrings, flavoured with onion, gherkin and spices) are a great storecupboard ingredient. In this nutritious main-dish salad, the silver skins of the herrings look sensational with colourful cubes of beetroot, orange segments, radishes and salad leaves. Serve with rye bread.

Serves 4

2 jars of rollmops, about 260 g each, drained of brine

2 oranges

115 g (4 oz) mixed salad leaves, such as frisée, radicchio, rocket, mizuna, watercress and red mustard

3 celery sticks, cut into fine sticks about 6 cm (2½ in) long

8 radishes, sliced

200 g (7 oz) peeled cooked beetroot (2–3 medium-sized or 6 small beetroot), cubed

Dill dressing

4 tbsp mayonnaise

4 tbsp plain low-fat yogurt

2 tbsp chopped fresh dill

Preparation time: 10 minutes

Each serving provides

kcal 440, **protein** 25 g, **fat** 26 g (of which saturated fat 2 g), **carbohydrate** 27 g (of which sugars 26 g), **fibre** 3 g

✓✓✓	C
✓✓	folate
✓	B$_2$, B$_6$, calcium, potassium

1 Slice the rollmops in half widthways, keeping them in rolls with onion and gherkin inside. Reserve any extra onion and gherkin.

2 Cut the peel and pith from the oranges with a sharp knife, then cut between the membrane to release the segments.

3 Put the salad leaves in a large bowl and toss with the celery, radishes and the reserved onion and gherkin from the rollmops. Add the beetroot cubes. Scatter the rollmops and orange segments over the salad.

4 Combine the ingredients for the dressing in a small bowl. Serve the salad with the dressing handed separately, for spooning over the salad at the table.

Some more ideas

● For a more substantial salad, add 450 g (1 lb) lightly boiled cubes of potato.

● For a smoked trout, tomato and apple salad, use 250 g (8½ oz) skinless smoked trout fillets, broken into pieces, in place of the rollmops. Combine the salad leaves and radishes with ½ cucumber, cut into thin sticks, 125 g (4½ oz) cherry tomatoes, halved, and 2 crisp apples, cored and sliced. Omit the celery, oranges and beetroot. Instead of dill in the dressing, flavour it with the grated zest of 1 lemon and 2–3 tbsp snipped fresh chives.

● Smoked mackerel or kipper fillets or canned tuna in spring water, drained, can be used in place of the herring or trout.

● Dress the salad with a light vinaigrette made by whisking together 4 tbsp extra virgin olive oil, 1 tbsp lemon juice, ½ tsp wholegrain mustard, 2 tbsp snipped fresh chives and seasoning to taste.

Plus points

● Beetroot is a good source of folate, which is needed during the early stages of pregnancy to reduce the risk of spina bifida. It is also rich in potassium, a good intake of which can help to balance the adverse effect of a high salt intake on blood pressure.

● Herring is an excellent source of omega-3 fatty acids, which are believed to help protect against heart disease and thrombosis.

Seared tuna and bean salad

This healthy version of a classic salad is perfect for warm weather eating. Fresh tuna is quickly cooked in a hot pan so the outside is lightly browned, leaving the inside pink, moist and full of flavour, and then served on a cannellini bean and red pepper salad. Warm ciabatta bread, thickly sliced, is the best accompaniment.

Serves 4

400 g (14 oz) piece tuna steak, about 5 cm (2 in) thick
4 tbsp extra virgin olive oil
1 tbsp lemon juice, or to taste
1 garlic clove, crushed
1 tbsp Dijon mustard
1 can cannellini beans, about 410 g, drained and rinsed
1 small red onion, thinly sliced
2 red peppers, seeded and thinly sliced
½ cucumber, about 225 g (8 oz)
100 g (3½ oz) watercress
salt and pepper
lemon wedges to serve

Preparation and cooking time: 30 minutes

Each serving provides

kcal 380, **protein** 32 g, **fat** 17 g (of which saturated fat 3 g), **carbohydrate** 26 g (of which sugars 11 g), **fibre** 9 g

✓✓✓	A, B$_6$, B$_{12}$, C, selenium
✓✓	B$_1$, niacin, iron
✓	E, folate, copper, potassium, zinc

1 Brush a ridged cast-iron grill pan or heavy frying pan (preferably cast-iron) with a little oil and heat over a moderate heat. Season the tuna steak on both sides with coarsely ground black pepper.

2 Sear the fish in the hot pan over a moderately high heat for 4 minutes on each side – the outside should be browned and criss-crossed with dark lines from the grill pan, while the inside should be light pink in the centre. Take care not to overcook the tuna or it will become tough and dry. Remove from the pan and leave to rest while preparing the rest of the salad.

3 Mix together the oil, lemon juice, garlic and mustard in a salad bowl. Season with salt and pepper to taste and add more lemon juice, if needed. Add the cannellini beans, onion and peppers to the bowl. Cut the cucumber lengthways into quarters, then cut the quarters across into 1 cm (½ in) slices. Add them to the salad bowl together with the watercress. Toss the salad gently to mix.

4 Cut the tuna into slices about 1 cm (½ in) thick. Arrange the slices on top of the salad and spoon up a little of the dressing over the fish. Serve with lemon wedges.

Another idea

● For a warm chicken and bean salad, use 500 g (1 lb 2 oz) skinless boneless chicken breasts (fillets). Cook in the hot pan for 18–20 minutes, turning frequently, until the chicken is cooked through. Leave to cool while you make the salad. Instead of cannellini beans, watercress and cucumber, use 1 can borlotti beans, about 400 g, drained and rinsed, 100 g (3½ oz) baby leaf spinach or rocket, and 250 g (8½ oz) cherry tomatoes, halved, with the onion and peppers. Slice the chicken, arrange on the salad and spoon over the dressing.

Plus points

● The health benefits of eating watercress have been acknowledged for many centuries. Along with other dark green, leafy vegetables, it provides good amounts of several vitamins and minerals including vitamin C, vitamin E, carotenoid compounds and the B vitamins folate, niacin and vitamin B$_6$.

● Canned beans are a useful source of iron, and the vitamin C from the watercress and peppers will help enhance its absorption.

Potato salad with bresaola and horseradish dressing

Everyone loves potato salad, but it can be high in calories and fat. This lower-fat version is made with a light fromage frais and yogurt dressing flavoured with horseradish. Slice the potatoes to reduce cooking time, toss in the dressing while still warm and serve attractively garnished with bresaola (Italian dried beef).

Serves 4

600 g (1 lb 5 oz) baby new potatoes, scrubbed and thickly sliced

115 g (4 oz) button mushrooms, thinly sliced

1 red onion, halved and thinly sliced

150 g (5½ oz) endive and radicchio salad or mixed salad leaves

75 g (2½ oz) watercress

8 slices bresaola, about 90 g (3¼ oz) in total

paprika to garnish

Dressing

6 tbsp fromage frais

6 tbsp plain low-fat yogurt

1 tbsp creamed horseradish

salt and pepper

Preparation and cooking time: 25 minutes

Each serving provides

kcal 280, **protein** 21 g, **fat** 10 g (of which saturated fat 6 g), **carbohydrate** 36 g (of which sugars 12 g), **fibre** 3 g

✓✓✓	B₆, C
✓✓	A, B₁₂, calcium, potassium
✓	B₂, folate, iron, zinc

1 Cook the potatoes in a saucepan of boiling water for 7–8 minutes or until just tender.

2 Meanwhile, make the dressing by mixing together the fromage frais, yogurt, horseradish, and salt and pepper to taste in a large bowl.

3 Drain the cooked potatoes and add them to the dressing together with the mushrooms and three-quarters of the onion. Toss together gently.

4 Tear any large salad leaves into bite-sized pieces. Divide the leaves and watercress among 4 serving plates and spoon the potato salad on top. Halve the slices of bresaola and arrange them on the potatoes. Sprinkle with the remaining onion slices and a little paprika. Serve while the potatoes are still warm.

Some more ideas

• Replace the mushrooms with sliced celery, and the red onion with 4–5 sliced spring onions.

• For a potato and steak salad, replace the horseradish in the dressing with 2 tsp wholegrain mustard and 2 crushed garlic cloves. Spoon the potato salad onto a serving plate lined with 8 small sliced tomatoes, about 400 g (14 oz) in total. Heat 1 tbsp extra virgin olive oil in a ridged grill pan, add 4 wafer-thin slices of sandwich steak, about 225 g (8 oz) in total, and fry for 1 minute on each side for medium, or 2 minutes on each side for well done. Cut into strips and arrange on the potatoes. Finish with onion slices and paprika as in the main recipe.

• Instead of bresaola, the salad can be garnished with Parma ham, wafer-thin smoked ham or salami. Strips of grilled back bacon or flaked smoked mackerel also work well.

• The potato salad can be made in advance and chilled, then spooned onto the salad leaves just before serving.

Plus points

• Bresaola is an Italian speciality, made by air-drying lean tender cuts of beef which is then matured for several months. As it is cut into wafer-thin slices, rather like Parma ham, a little goes a long way, keeping each serving low in calories and fat.

• Most salad leaves are a good source of folate, but, in general, bitter leaves such as endive and radicchio tend to have a higher nutrient content than mild leaves.

Butter bean dip with crudités

This quick and tasty dip is made from canned butter beans puréed with sun-dried tomato paste, garlic and fresh basil leaves. Served with sesame seed breadsticks, pitta bread and a selection of crunchy vegetables for dipping, it makes a nutritious lunch for 6 or a starter for 8.

Serves 6

1 can butter beans, about 410 g, drained and rinsed

150 g (5½ oz) Greek-style yogurt

1–2 garlic cloves, crushed

2 tbsp sun-dried tomato paste

few drops of Tabasco sauce

1 tsp lemon juice

10 g (¼ oz) fresh basil leaves

salt and pepper

To serve

225 g (8 oz) baby carrots

250 g (8½ oz) baby corn, blanched for 1 minute and drained, then halved lengthways, if wished

1 small red pepper, seeded and cut into strips

1 small yellow pepper, seeded and cut into strips

4 celery sticks, cut into 7.5 cm (3 in) strips

4 pitta breads

125 g (4½ oz) sesame seed breadsticks

Preparation time: about 15 minutes

Each serving provides (V)

kcal 505, protein 22 g, fat 8 g (of which saturated fat 4 g), carbohydrate 91 g (of which sugars 15 g), fibre 10 g

✓✓✓	A, C
✓✓	B₁, B₆, folate, copper, iron
✓	B₂, E, niacin, potassium, zinc

1 Place the butter beans, yogurt, garlic, tomato paste, Tabasco sauce and lemon juice in a food processor or blender. Reserve one basil leaf for garnishing, and add the rest to the food processor or blender. Blend to a smooth purée, scraping down the sides of the container once or twice. Season with salt and pepper to taste. Spoon into a bowl and garnish with the reserved basil leaf. Cover and chill while preparing the crudités.

2 Preheat the grill. Prepare all the vegetables and arrange them on a large serving platter. Warm the pittas under the grill for 1–2 minutes, then cut into wedges. Add to the vegetable platter with the sesame breadsticks. Serve with the dip.

Some more ideas

● Use deliciously creamy 0%-fat Greek-style yogurt for a lower-fat dip.

● For a saffron and lime dip, pour 1 tsp boiling water over a small pinch of saffron threads and leave to soak for 5 minutes. Stir the liquid into 200 g (7 oz) fromage frais (virtually fat-free, if you prefer) and add 3 tbsp mayonnaise, 1 tsp fresh lime juice, ½ crushed garlic clove and ½ tsp coarsely ground mixed red and black peppercorns. Serve with the vegetable crudités and bread.

Plus points

● Using yogurt in a dip, rather than oil or mayonnaise, helps to boost the calcium content – all dairy products are an excellent source of calcium. Because calcium is contained in the non-creamy portion of milk, it remains in reduced-fat dairy products after the fat has been removed, so using 0%-fat Greek-style yogurt will still provide calcium.

● Butter beans and raw vegetables are full of dietary fibre, essential for a healthy digestive system.

● Some studies have shown that eating raw garlic can help to reduce the cholesterol level in the blood.

● Colourful vegetables such as red and yellow peppers, tomatoes and sweetcorn contain plenty of beta-carotene, which the body can convert to vitamin A, and vitamin C, needed for healthy bones and tissues. Beta-carotene and vitamin C are also powerful antioxidants, which means they help to protect the body's cells from the damaging effects of free radicals.

for maximum vitality

Papaya and avocado salad

This refreshing salad with a hint of spice will convert anyone wary of mixing fruit with raw vegetables. Starting with a base of crisp lettuce, slices of orange or yellow pepper are layered with avocado and papaya. Toasted pumpkin seeds add protein and crunch. Serve with mixed grain or pumpkin bread for a light lunch.

Serves 4

1 romaine or cos lettuce heart, about 170 g (6 oz)

2 spring onions, thinly sliced

1 large orange or yellow pepper, quartered and seeded

1 large avocado, about 200 g (7 oz)

1 large papaya, about 500 g (1 lb 2 oz)

6 tbsp pumpkin seeds

Spicy dressing

juice of 1 lime

3 tbsp extra virgin olive oil

good pinch of paprika

good pinch of ground cumin

1 tsp light soft brown sugar

Preparation time: 12 minutes

1 Shred the lettuce leaves and put them in a large shallow dish or 4 individual dishes. Sprinkle the spring onions over the lettuce.

2 Cut the pepper quarters across into thin strips and arrange them in the dish. Halve, stone and peel the avocado, and cut into 5 mm (¼ in) slices across the width. Peel, halve and seed the papaya, and cut into 5 mm (¼ in) slices across the width. Scatter the avocado and papaya slices over the pepper strips.

3 Whisk all the dressing ingredients together and pour over the salad. Heat a small heavy saucepan, add the pumpkin seeds and toss them in the pan to toast them lightly. Sprinkle the seeds over the salad and serve.

Some more ideas

● For a mango and avocado salad with a chilli dressing, use mango instead of papaya, and a red pepper instead of orange or yellow. Instead of paprika and cumin in the dressing, add a small fresh red or green chilli, seeded and finely chopped, and the grated zest of 1 lime. Top the salad with 100 g (3½ oz) toasted cashew nuts instead of pumpkin seeds.

● For a fennel, orange and melon salad, thinly slice 1 small fennel bulb and mix with the segments from 2 oranges and ½ Galia or Ogen melon, cut into slivers. Arrange on a bed of rocket and scatter over 8 halved black olives.

Plus points

● Peppers are well known to be a rich source of vitamin C, and serving them raw in a salad makes more of this vitamin available than if they were cooked. They also contain high levels of beta-carotene and other members of the carotene family, such as capsanthin and zeaxanthin. All of these work as antioxidants, helping to prevent cancers, heart disease, strokes and cataracts.

● Papaya provides vitamin C and protective carotenes as well as calcium, iron and zinc.

● Pumpkin seeds have a lot to offer: protein, fibre, unsaturated fat, vitamin E and some B vitamins, as well as iron for healthy blood, magnesium for maintaining healthy body cells and zinc for growth and development.

Each serving provides Ⓥ

kcal 240, **protein** 2 g, **fat** 18 g (of which saturated fat 3 g), **carbohydrate** 17 g (of which sugars 17 g), **fibre** 5 g

✓✓✓	A, C
✓✓	B₆, E
✓	B₁, B₂, copper, iron, potassium

for maximum vitality

Braised duck with crunchy Oriental salad

Braising boneless duck breasts in red wine with garlic and ginger, plus a little redcurrant jelly for sweetness, produces moist, tender and flavoursome meat. The duck is cut into strips and served on a colourful mixture of crisp raw vegetables and fruit. Rice cakes would be an interesting Oriental-style accompaniment.

Serves 4

3 boneless duck breasts, about 525 g
  (1 lb 3 oz) in total
120 ml (4 fl oz) red wine
1 tbsp redcurrant jelly
1 tsp bottled chopped garlic in oil, drained
1 tsp bottled chopped root ginger in oil,
  drained
2 tbsp extra virgin olive oil
2 tsp balsamic or sherry vinegar
2 oranges
225 g (8 oz) red cabbage, finely shredded
¼ head of Chinese leaves, shredded
150 g (5½ oz) beansprouts
85 g (3 oz) watercress
1 can water chestnuts, about 220 g, drained
  and sliced
salt and pepper

Preparation and cooking time: 30 minutes

Each serving provides

kcal 334, **protein** 31 g, **fat** 12 g (of which saturated fat 3 g), **carbohydrate** 20 g (of which sugars 16 g), **fibre** 4 g

✓✓✓	B₆, B₁₂, C
✓✓	B₁, B₂, folate, niacin, copper, iron, potassium, zinc
✓	A, calcium

1 Preheat the oven to 220°C (425°F, gas mark 7). Remove all the skin and fat from the duck breasts. Place them in an ovenproof dish, pour over the wine and add the redcurrant jelly, garlic and ginger. Place the dish in the oven and cook the duck for 20–25 minutes or until tender.

2 Meanwhile, mix together the oil, vinegar and salt and pepper to taste in a large salad bowl. Cut the peel and pith from the oranges with a sharp knife and, holding each orange over the bowl to catch the juice, cut between the membrane to release the segments. Add them to the bowl. Add the red cabbage, Chinese leaves, beansprouts, watercress (reserving a few sprigs for garnishing) and water chestnuts. Toss well to coat everything with the dressing.

3 Remove the duck from the oven and transfer it to a warm plate. Pour the cooking liquid into a saucepan. Boil the liquid rapidly for 1–2 minutes to reduce slightly, while cutting the duck diagonally across the grain into neat slices. Pour the wine sauce over the salad and toss together. Pile the slices of duck on top, garnish with the reserved sprigs of watercress and serve.

Plus points

● All types of cabbage are rich in a range of vitamins, minerals and cancer-fighting phytochemicals.

● Duck is higher in fat than other poultry; however, removing the skin and all visible fat reduces the fat content considerably. The meat is rich in minerals, providing iron and zinc, as well as B vitamins.

● This salad contains a wide selection of different vegetables served raw, which preserves their vitamin value.

● Red wine is a rich source of flavonols, which are powerful antioxidants.

for maximum vitality

Some more ideas

- If fresh redcurrants are available, add a handful to the salad for extra vitamins and flavour.
- For a sesame roast pork salad, use 450 g (1 lb) pork fillet (tenderloin). Mix together 1 tbsp groundnut oil, 2 tbsp hoisin sauce and 1 tsp five-spice powder, and spoon the mixture over the pork. Sprinkle with 1 tsp sesame seeds. Roast in a preheated 180°C (350°F, gas mark 4) oven for 20–25 minutes. Make the salad using 1 cos lettuce, shredded, 1 orange pepper, seeded and chopped, 125 g (4½ oz) sliced mushrooms, 125 g (4½ oz) mange-tout, and the sliced water chestnuts. Toss the salad with 1 tbsp each olive oil and toasted sesame oil. Serve with the sliced pork on top.
- Other vegetables that could be added to the salad are lightly cooked baby corn, sliced raw courgettes or steamed asparagus spears.
- Sprinkle the salad with toasted cashew nuts.

Melon, feta and orange salad

Here, the classic starter of melon and Parma ham is transformed into a tempting main-dish salad with the addition of feta cheese, cherry tomatoes, cucumber and oranges. Serve for lunch, with warm ciabatta bread to mop up the juices, or as a starter for 6 people.

Serves 4

2 oranges

½ honeydew melon, peeled, seeded and sliced

115 g (4 oz) cherry tomatoes, halved

85 g (3 oz) stoned black olives

½ small cucumber, diced

4 spring onions, thinly sliced

6 slices of Parma ham, about 80 g (2¾ oz) in total, trimmed of all fat and cut into strips

100 g (3½ oz) feta cheese, roughly broken into pieces

Orange and basil dressing

½ tsp grated orange zest

4 tbsp orange juice

2 tbsp extra virgin olive oil

1 tsp toasted sesame oil

6 fresh basil leaves, shredded

salt and pepper

Preparation time: 20–25 minutes

1 Make the dressing first. Mix the orange zest and juice with the olive oil, sesame oil and basil in a large salad bowl. Season with salt and pepper to taste.

2 Cut the peel and pith away from the oranges with a sharp knife. Holding them over the salad bowl to catch the juice, cut between the membrane to release the orange segments. Add the segments to the bowl.

3 Add the melon, tomatoes, olives, cucumber, spring onions and Parma ham. Toss until the ingredients are well blended and coated in dressing. Scatter the feta cheese over the top and serve.

Some more ideas

• To make a melon and fresh pineapple salad with cottage cheese, mix the melon, tomato and cucumber with ½ pineapple, peeled, cored and chopped, and 3 shallots, thinly sliced. Make a lime dressing by mixing ½ tsp grated lime zest and 2 tbsp lime juice with 2 tbsp sunflower oil and 1 tsp clear honey. Season to taste. Stir the dressing into the melon mixture and pile onto 4 plates. Spoon 75 g (2½ oz) plain cottage cheese on top of each salad and scatter over roasted, chopped macadamia nuts, 50 g (1¾ oz) in total. Garnish generously with small sprigs of watercress.

• Substitute Serrano ham from Spain or smoky Black Forest ham for the Parma ham.

• As an alternative to honeydew melon, try other varieties such as Ogen or Charentais or a wedge of watermelon.

Plus points

• Although feta cheese is high in fat and salt, it is an excellent source of calcium, and because it has a strong flavour a little goes a long way. Calcium in dairy products is much more easily absorbed by the body than calcium from other foods.

• Only 1 in 4 people in the UK drink enough water or other fluid. Foods that have a high water content, such as melon and cucumber, are an easy way of increasing fluid intake.

Each serving provides

kcal 260, **protein** 13 g, **fat** 16 g (of which saturated fat 6 g), **carbohydrate** 16 g (of which sugars 16 g), **fibre** 3 g

✓✓✓	C
✓✓	B$_6$, B$_{12}$, calcium
✓	A, B$_1$, E, folate, potassium

for maximum vitality

Family Meals in Minutes

Well-balanced fast food for all the family

Keep a well-stocked storecupboard, plus a cleverly organised fridge and freezer, and you can have tempting and nutritious meals on the table in less than 30 minutes. A good stock of pasta, rice and grains provides the basis for all kinds of speedy meals. Enjoy a delicious Chinese-style stir-fry with beef and mushrooms served with noodles, or spicy chicken drumsticks with Creole rice. Eggs provide the basis for a delicious spinach and potato frittata. And canned tuna and tomatoes on ready-made thick pizza bases make a family feast.

Hoisin beef stir-fry

For a quick special supper for 2, try this colourful stir-fry of thin strips of tender steak with fresh ginger, button mushrooms, red peppers and crisp mange-tout, served on Chinese egg noodles. Hoisin sauce, a sweet Chinese barbecue sauce made from soya and red beans, gives the stir-fry a rich flavour.

Serves 2

2 sheets medium Chinese egg noodles, about 170 g (6 oz) in total
1 tbsp sunflower oil
2 large garlic cloves, cut into shreds
1 tsp grated fresh root ginger
1 large red pepper, seeded and thinly sliced
125 g (4½ oz) baby button mushrooms, halved
1 sirloin steak, about 200 g (7 oz), trimmed of fat and cut into thin strips
85 g (3 oz) mange-tout, halved lengthways
4 spring onions, cut into chunky lengths
3 tbsp hoisin sauce
1 tbsp light soy sauce
1 tsp toasted sesame oil (optional)
shredded spring onion to garnish

Preparation time: 15 minutes
Cooking time: 6 minutes

Each serving provides

kcal 620, protein 38 g, fat 20 g (of which saturated fat 5 g), carbohydrate 76 g (of which sugars 11 g), fibre 6 g

✓✓✓	A, B₆, B₁₂, C, copper, iron, zinc
✓✓	B₁, B₂, E, folate, niacin, potassium
✓	calcium, selenium

1 Put the noodles in a bowl, cover with boiling water and leave to soak for 5 minutes, or according to the packet instructions.

2 Meanwhile, heat the sunflower oil in a wok or large frying pan, add the garlic and ginger, and cook very briefly to release their flavour. Toss in the red pepper and mushrooms, then stir-fry over a high heat for 2–3 minutes or until starting to soften.

3 Add the strips of steak, mange-tout and spring onions, and stir-fry for a further 1–2 minutes or until the meat just turns from pink to brown.

4 Mix in the hoisin and soy sauces and stir well until bubbling, then drizzle in the sesame oil, if using. Drain the noodles. Serve the stir-fry on the noodles, garnished with shredded spring onion.

Some more ideas

● Use skinless boneless chicken breasts (fillets) or pork fillet (tenderloin) instead of steak.

● To make turkey pan-fry with fresh basil and chilli, use 200 g (7 oz) skinless turkey breast steaks, cut into thin strips. Mix together 2 tbsp fish sauce, 2 tbsp light soy sauce, 1 tsp cornflour and 2 tsp light soft brown sugar. Instead of ginger, stir-fry a fresh red chilli, seeded and sliced, with the garlic. Add the turkey with the mange-tout and spring onions and stir-fry for about 4 minutes. Add 1 tsp ground coriander and stir well, then pour in the fish sauce mixture and stir until lightly thickened. Toss in 2 tbsp shredded fresh basil, then serve, with the noodles or jasmine rice.

Plus points

● Beef has received a great deal of bad press in recent years. However, it has nutritional benefits that should not be overlooked: in common with other red meats, beef is an excellent source of zinc and a good source of iron. The iron in meat is much more easily absorbed by the body than iron from vegetable sources.

● As a result of modern breeding techniques beef is now much leaner than it used to be – lean cuts can contain less than 3% fat.

● Red peppers offer an impressive arsenal of disease-fighting chemicals. In addition to vitamin C and beta-carotene, they also contain two other important phytochemicals, lutein and zeaxanthin. Studies suggest that these can help to protect against the eye disease, age-related macular degeneration (AMD), which affects 20% of people over the age of 65 and is the leading cause of blindness in the Western world.

Spicy sausage paprikash

Here, good-quality pork sausages are cooked in a tasty sauce with lots of colourful vegetables – red onions, carrots, green peppers and celery. The dish is finished with paprika and soured cream before serving on a bed of ribbon noodles. A fresh green salad is a good partner.

Serves 4

1 tbsp sunflower oil

400 g (14 oz) high-meat-content premium pork sausages

2 red onions, thinly sliced

2 garlic cloves, crushed

4 baby carrots, halved

2 green peppers, seeded and cut into 2.5 cm (1 in) dice

4 celery sticks, thinly sliced

2 tsp plain flour

325 ml (10½ fl oz) vegetable stock

¼–½ tsp crushed dried chillies

good pinch of dried marjoram

400 g (14 oz) pappardelle or other wide flat noodles

salt and pepper

To finish

1 tbsp paprika

2 tbsp soured cream

Preparation and cooking time: 30 minutes

Each serving provides

kcal 655, **protein** 27 g, **fat** 22 g (of which saturated fat 7 g), **carbohydrate** 92 g (of which sugars 11 g), **fibre** 7 g

✓✓✓	A, C
✓✓	B₆, B₁₂, copper, iron, zinc
✓	B₁, B₂, E, folate, niacin, calcium, potassium

1 Heat the sunflower oil in a large, deep frying pan that has a lid, or in a flameproof casserole. Add the sausages and quickly brown on all sides over a moderately high heat. Remove the sausages from the pan with kitchen tongs and leave to cool slightly on a board. Pour off all but 1 tbsp of the fat remaining in the pan.

2 Add the onions and garlic to the pan and stir well, then cover, reduce the heat and cook gently for 5 minutes. Add the carrots, peppers and celery and stir well to mix. Stir in the flour, then gradually mix in the stock. Bring to the boil, stirring.

3 Cut the sausages into thick slices and return them to the pan. Stir in the crushed chillies and marjoram, and season with salt and pepper to taste. Cover and simmer gently for 15 minutes, stirring occasionally.

4 Meanwhile, cook the pappardelle in boiling water for 10–12 minutes, or according to the packet instructions, until al dente. Drain and keep warm.

5 Sprinkle the paprika over the sausage mixture and stir in. Taste and add more crushed chillies or seasoning, if liked. Drizzle the soured cream over the top of the sausage mixture and serve, with the noodles.

Some more ideas

● Replace the carrots with 200 g (7 oz) small button mushrooms.

● For chicken paprikash, use 8 skinless boneless chicken thighs, about 675 g (1½ lb) in total. Cut each thigh in half before browning, and cook for 20–25 minutes. Serve with boiled or steamed new potatoes.

● For a traditional veal paprikash, use 400 g (14 oz) diced lean boneless veal, and cook for 20–25 minutes in the sauce.

Plus points

● Sausages with a high lean meat content are the best healthy choice. They are a good source of protein and iron.

● Carrots are rich in beta-carotene. Cooking makes them more nutritious as the body is able to convert more of their beta-carotene into vitamin A.

● Pasta is an excellent source of starchy carbohydrate and it is low in fat. It also contains valuable vitamins, in particular the water-soluble B vitamins that we need to take in regularly.

Greek lamb kebabs

Cubes of lamb flavoured with a mixture of garlic, lemon and fresh oregano are cooked on skewers and served with a Greek-style tomato and cabbage salad and pitta bread for a deliciously aromatic main dish.

Serves 4

1 tbsp extra virgin olive oil

2 large garlic cloves, crushed

juice of ½ lemon

1 tbsp chopped fresh oregano

450 g (1 lb) boneless leg of lamb, trimmed of
   all fat and cut into 2.5 cm (1 in) cubes

salt and pepper

Greek-style salad

6 tomatoes, thickly sliced

1 red onion, finely chopped

1 baby white cabbage, about 225 g (8 oz),
   core removed and thinly shredded

4 tbsp chopped fresh mint

¼ cucumber, halved and thinly sliced

juice of ½ lemon

1 tbsp extra virgin olive oil

To serve

4 pitta breads, cut into triangles

Greek-style yogurt (optional)

Preparation and cooking time: 30 minutes

Each serving provides

kcal 470, **protein** 32 g, **fat** 16 g (of which saturated fat 5 g), **carbohydrate** 52 g (of which sugars 10 g), **fibre** 5 g

✓✓✓	B$_{12}$, C
✓✓	A, B$_6$, E, iron, zinc
✓	B$_1$, folate, niacin, potassium

1 Preheat the grill or heat a ridged cast-iron grill pan. Put the olive oil, garlic, lemon juice and chopped oregano in a bowl and stir to mix together. Add the cubes of lamb and turn until very well coated. Thread the cubes onto 4 skewers.

2 Cook the lamb under the grill or on the grill pan for 7–8 minutes or until tender, turning frequently. Towards the end of cooking, warm the pitta bread under the grill or on the grill pan.

3 Meanwhile, make the salad. Put all the ingredients in a salad bowl and season with salt and pepper to taste. Toss together gently.

4 Serve the kebabs with the salad, pitta bread and yogurt.

Another idea

● To make chilli beef kebabs, use 4 beef fillet or sirloin steaks, about 400 g (14 oz) in total, cut into 2.5 cm (1 in) cubes. Mix together 1 tsp chilli powder, ¼ tsp ground cumin, 1 tbsp extra virgin olive oil, 2 large garlic cloves, crushed, the juice of ½ lime and seasoning to taste. Coat the steak cubes on all sides with the spice mixture, then thread onto 4 skewers. Cook with 1 large sliced onion under the grill or on the ridged grill pan for 4–6 minutes or until tender, turning frequently. Take the skewers from the pan and continue cooking the onion until tender. Meanwhile, to make the salad, mix 1 can red kidney beans, about 410 g, drained and rinsed, with 1 large diced avocado, the juice of 1 lime, 1½ tbsp extra virgin olive oil, ½ red onion, very finely chopped, 1 fresh green chilli, seeded and finely chopped, 300 g (10½ oz) cherry tomatoes, halved, and 15 g (½ oz) chopped fresh coriander. Season to taste and add a pinch of caster sugar. Remove the steak from the skewers and divide with the onion among 8 warmed flour tortillas. Add 1 tbsp bottled Caesar salad dressing and some of the salad to each tortilla, and roll up into wraps. Serve with the rest of the salad.

Plus points

● Lamb is a rich source of B vitamins, needed for a healthy nervous system. It is also a good source of zinc and iron.

● Cabbage belongs to a family of vegetables that contain a number of different phytochemicals that may help to protect against breast cancer. They are also a good source of vitamin C and among the richest vegetable sources of folate.

● Onions, along with chicory, leeks, garlic, Jerusalem artichokes, asparagus, barley and bananas, contain a type of dietary fibre called fructoligosaccharides (FOS). This is believed to stimulate the growth of friendly bacteria in the gut while inhibiting the growth of bad bacteria.

Pork steaks with mustard sauce

This delectable dish is surprisingly quick and easy to make, and can turn a family dinner into a celebration. Serve with boiled new potatoes sprinkled with chives, carrots and shredded Savoy cabbage. The carrots can be steamed over the pan of potatoes, with the cabbage added after a few minutes.

Serves 4

1 tsp extra virgin olive oil

4 boneless pork loin steaks or chops, 1.5–2 cm (⅝–¾ in) thick, about 550 g (1¼ lb) in total, trimmed of all fat

4 tbsp dry white wine or vermouth

1 garlic clove, finely chopped

170 ml (6 fl oz) chicken or vegetable stock

2 tsp cornflour mixed with 1 tbsp water

120 ml (4 fl oz) crème fraîche

1 tbsp Dijon mustard

1 tbsp chopped fresh tarragon

salt and pepper

fresh chives to garnish

Preparation and cooking time: 30 minutes

Each serving provides

kcal 325, **protein** 31 g, **fat** 20 g (of which saturated fat 7 g), **carbohydrate** 4 g (of which sugars 1 g), **fibre** 0 g

✓✓✓	B_1
✓✓	B_6, B_{12}, niacin, zinc
✓	B_2, iron, selenium

1 Heat the oil in a non-stick frying pan over a moderately high heat. Add the pork steaks and fry for 3 minutes on each side or until well browned. Remove the pork steaks to a plate.

2 Add the wine or vermouth to the frying pan with the garlic and let it bubble briefly, then pour in the stock and boil for 2 minutes. Stir together the cornflour mixture and crème fraîche until smooth. Add to the hot cooking liquid, stirring well. Simmer gently for 2 minutes, stirring constantly, until thickened and smooth. Stir in the mustard and tarragon, and season with salt and pepper to taste.

3 Return the pork steaks to the sauce. Reduce the heat to low, cover the pan and cook for 4–5 minutes or until the steaks are cooked through.

4 Arrange the pork steaks on warm plates and spoon the sauce over. Garnish with chives and serve at once.

Another idea

● Grill the steaks or chops and serve with a cabbage, apple and onion braise. Brush the steaks with a little extra virgin olive oil and cook under a preheated moderate grill for about 7 minutes on each side or until tender and well browned. Meanwhile, heat 1 tbsp extra virgin olive oil in a large, deep frying pan over a moderate heat and add 1 large red onion, sliced, 2 apples, cored and cut in eighths, and 450 g (1 lb) shredded Savoy cabbage (about ½ head). Toss to mix well, then cover and cook for about 4 minutes or until lightly browned, stirring occasionally. Moisten with 3–4 tbsp apple juice and continue cooking, covered, until wilted and just tender, stirring frequently.

Plus points

● In the past, pork had a reputation for being rather fatty, but this is no longer the case. Over the last 20 years, in response to consumer demands for leaner meat, farmers have been breeding leaner pigs. While now containing considerably less fat, pork also contains higher levels of the 'good' polyunsaturated fats. The average fat content of lean pork is less than 3%, which is much the same as that of a chicken breast.

● Garlic was first used as a medicine at least 4000 years ago – the ancient Egyptians used it to treat infections and headaches, and Roman soldiers who marched across Europe to Britain wedged garlic cloves between their toes to help prevent athlete's foot. Allicin, the compound that gives garlic its characteristic smell and taste, acts as a powerful antibiotic and has anti-viral and anti-fungal properties.

Lamb burgers with fruity relish

The advantage of making your own burgers is that you know exactly what's in them – and they can look and taste better than any takeaway while being a really healthy meal. An orange and raspberry relish adds a lovely fresh flavour to these juicy lamb burgers as well as lots of vitamins. Serve with a green or mixed salad.

Serves 4

400 g (14 oz) lean minced lamb

1 carrot, about 125 g (4½ oz), grated

1 small onion, finely chopped

50 g (1¾ oz) fresh wholemeal breadcrumbs

pinch of freshly grated nutmeg

2 tsp fresh thyme leaves or 1 tsp dried thyme

1 large egg, beaten

2 tsp extra virgin olive oil

4 wholemeal baps, weighing about
    55 g (2 oz) each

salt and pepper

shredded lettuce to garnish

Orange and raspberry relish

1 orange

100 g (3½ oz) fresh or thawed frozen
    raspberries

2 tsp demerara sugar

Preparation and cooking time: 30 minutes

Each serving provides

kcal 390, **protein** 29 g, **fat** 13 g (of which saturated fat 5 g), **carbohydrate** 40 g (of which sugars 12 g), **fibre** 6 g

✓✓✓	A, B$_{12}$
✓✓	B$_1$, B$_6$, C, niacin, copper, iron, selenium, zinc
✓	B$_2$, folate, calcium, potassium

1 Preheat the grill. Put the lamb into a large bowl. Add the carrot, onion, breadcrumbs, nutmeg and thyme, and season with salt and pepper to taste. Mix roughly with a spoon. Add the egg and use your hands to mix the ingredients together thoroughly.

2 Divide the mixture into 4 and shape each portion into a burger about 10–12 cm (4–5 in) in diameter, or about 2.5 cm (1 in) bigger than the diameter of the baps. Brush both sides of the burgers with oil, then put them in the grill pan. Cook for 4–5 minutes on each side, depending on thickness.

3 Meanwhile, make the relish. Cut the peel and pith from the orange with a sharp knife and, holding it over a bowl to catch the juice, cut between the membrane to release the segments. Roughly chop the segments and add them to the juice. Add the raspberries and sugar, lightly crushing the fruit with a fork to mix it together.

4 Split the baps and toast briefly under the grill. Put a lamb burger in each bap and add some lettuce to garnish and a good spoonful of relish. Serve with the remaining relish.

Another idea

● Make turkey burgers with an orange and summer fruit relish. Use minced turkey instead of lamb, and flavour with the zest of ½ lemon and 4 tbsp chopped parsley in place of the nutmeg and thyme; omit the breadcrumbs. Serve in toasted sesame buns, with rocket leaves and a relish made by simmering 100 g (3½ oz) frozen summer fruits for about 3 minutes or until thawed, and mixing with 1 tbsp caster sugar and the chopped orange.

Plus points

● Although lamb still tends to contain more fat than other meats, changes in breeding, feeding and butchery techniques mean that lean cuts only contain about one-third of the fat that they would have 20 years ago. More of the fat is monounsaturated, which is good news for healthy hearts.

● Using wholemeal baps instead of white ones doubles the amount of fibre. The bread also provides B-complex vitamins, iron and calcium.

● A fruity relish gives a huge bonus of protective antioxidants. It also provides useful amounts of potassium and fibre, especially from the raspberries.

family meals in minutes

Potato and bacon chowder

It's easy to make a nourishing supper based on ingredients you are likely to have on hand, such as onion, potatoes, parsnips, bacon and milk. Here they're turned into a hearty and satisfying soup, which is finished with a little vitamin-rich spinach. Serve the soup with chunks of crusty brown bread.

Serves 4

1 litre (1¾ pints) whole/creamy milk

1 tbsp extra virgin olive oil

55 g (2 oz) lean smoked back bacon, rinded and finely chopped

1 large onion, finely chopped

2 tbsp plain flour

400 g (14 oz) smooth thin-skinned potatoes, such as Desiree, scrubbed and finely diced

1 parsnip, about 150 g (5½ oz), grated

freshly grated nutmeg

115 g (4 oz) baby spinach leaves

salt and pepper

Preparation and cooking time: about 30 minutes

1 Bring the milk just to the boil in a saucepan. Meanwhile, in another large saucepan heat the oil over a moderately high heat. Add the bacon and onion and cook for 2 minutes, stirring frequently. Add the flour and stir to combine, then slowly add about one-quarter of the hot milk, stirring and scraping the bottom of the pan to mix in the flour. When the mixture thickens, stir in the remaining hot milk.

2 Add the potatoes and parsnip. Season with salt, pepper and nutmeg to taste and bring just to the boil, stirring occasionally. Adjust the heat so the soup bubbles gently. Half cover the pan and continue cooking for about 10 minutes or until the vegetables are nearly tender, stirring occasionally.

3 Stir in the spinach and continue cooking for 1–2 minutes or until the spinach has wilted. Taste the soup and adjust the seasoning, if necessary. Ladle into a warm tureen or individual bowls and serve at once.

Some more ideas

● Substitute 85 g (3 oz) rocket leaves or 150 g (5½ oz) cavolo nero (a leafy cabbage), thinly shredded, for the spinach. Cavolo nero will need 3–4 minutes cooking.

● Instead of bacon, use 150 g (5½ oz) frozen sweetcorn kernels, adding them with the potatoes and parsnip.

● For a smoked haddock chowder, omit the bacon and add 115 g (4 oz) skinless smoked haddock fillet with the potatoes and parsnip.

● Use a large carrot instead of the parsnip.

Plus points

● Dark green, leafy vegetables such as spinach and cavolo nero are a good source of several important phytochemicals, including indoles which some studies suggest may help to protect against breast cancer by inhibiting the action of the oestrogens that trigger the growth of tumours. They also contain sulphoraphane which is believed to stimulate the liver to produce cancer-fighting enzymes.

● Parsnips are a useful source of fibre, vitamin C and folate.

Each serving provides

kcal 355, **protein** 15 g, **fat** 14 g (of which saturated fat 7 g), **carbohydrate** 43 g (of which sugars 17 g), **fibre** 4 g

✓✓✓	B$_6$
✓✓	A, B$_1$, B$_{12}$, C, folate, calcium
✓	B$_2$, E, iron, potassium, zinc

Spicy drumsticks with Creole rice

These chicken drumsticks, coated in a mixture of dried herbs and spices, can be cooked under the grill in next to no time. They are served with Creole-style red beans and rice.

Serves 4

1 tbsp plain flour

1 tsp paprika

1 tsp ground black pepper

1 tsp garlic granules

½ tsp crushed dried chillies

1 tsp dried thyme

8 chicken drumsticks, about 675 g (1½ lb) in total, skinned

1 tbsp extra virgin olive oil

salt and pepper

sprigs of fresh parsley to garnish

Creole rice

1 tbsp extra virgin olive oil

1 onion, chopped

1 red pepper, seeded and diced

2 celery sticks, diced

170 g (6 oz) long-grain rice

600 ml (1 pint) vegetable stock

1 can red kidney beans, about 410 g, drained and rinsed

2 tbsp chopped parsley

Preparation and cooking time: 30 minutes

Each serving provides

kcal 480, **protein** 41 g, **fat** 11 g (of which saturated fat 2 g), **carbohydrate** 58 g (of which sugars 5 g), **fibre** 6 g

✓✓	D$_1$, D$_6$, niacin, iron, selenium, zinc
✓	folate, calcium, copper, potassium

1 Preheat the grill to moderate. Put the flour, paprika, pepper, garlic granules, chillies, thyme and a pinch of salt in a polythene bag and shake to mix. Make 2 slashes in each chicken drumstick and rub with the olive oil. Toss them one at a time in the bag to coat with the spice mixture. Shake off any excess mixture and place the chicken on the grill rack. Grill for 20–25 minutes or until golden and cooked through, turning often.

2 Meanwhile, make the Creole rice. Heat the oil in a large saucepan, add the onion, pepper and celery, and cook for 2 minutes or until softened. Stir in the rice, then add the stock and kidney beans. Bring to the boil. Cover and simmer gently for 15–20 minutes or until all the stock has been absorbed and the rice is tender.

3 Stir the chopped parsley into the rice and season with salt and pepper to taste. Spoon the rice onto 4 plates and place 2 drumsticks on top of each portion. Serve hot, garnished with sprigs of parsley.

Another idea

● For sticky chilli drumsticks, mix 2 tbsp tomato ketchup with 1 tbsp soy sauce and 2 tbsp sweet chilli sauce or paste. Rub onto the chicken drumsticks and grill as in the main recipe. Meanwhile, put 125 g (4½ oz) bulghur wheat in a heatproof bowl, pour over enough boiling water to cover and soak for 15–20 minutes. Squeeze out any excess water, then mix with 1 can borlotti beans, about 410 g, drained, ¼ diced cucumber, 2 chopped tomatoes, 2 tbsp chopped fresh mint and 2 tbsp chopped parsley. Add 1 tbsp lemon juice and 2 tbsp extra virgin olive oil and season to taste. Toss to mix. Serve with the sticky chilli drumsticks.

Plus points

● Chicken is an excellent source of protein and provides many B vitamins, in particular niacin. The dark meat contains twice as much iron and zinc as the light meat. Eaten without the skin, chicken is low in fat and what fat it does contain is mostly unsaturated.

● Celery contains a compound called phthalide, which is believed to help lower high blood pressure.

Moroccan chicken with couscous

Aromatic cumin, coriander and cinnamon give these chicken breasts a real Middle Eastern flavour, and serving them with chickpeas further enhances the ethnic theme. Courgettes and sugarsnap peas add a lovely splash of colour and all the benefits of fresh vegetables. Quick-cooking couscous makes the perfect accompaniment.

Serves 4

400 g (14 oz) skinless boneless chicken breasts (fillets)

2 tbsp extra virgin olive oil

1 large onion, finely chopped

2 garlic cloves, finely chopped

1 tsp ground cumin

1 tsp ground coriander

1 cinnamon stick

325 g (11½ oz) courgettes, halved lengthways and sliced

1 can chopped tomatoes, about 400 g

200 ml (7 fl oz) vegetable stock

250 g (8½ oz) couscous

400 ml (14 fl oz) boiling water

200 g (7 oz) sugarsnap peas

1 can chickpeas, about 410 g, drained and rinsed

10 g (¼ oz) butter

salt and pepper

chopped fresh coriander to garnish

Preparation and cooking time: 30 minutes

Each serving provides

kcal 500, **protein** 35 g, **fat** 15 g (of which saturated fat 4 g), **carbohydrate** 55 g (of which sugars 8 g), **fibre** 7 g

✓✓✓	B_6, C
✓✓	A, B_1, E, niacin, copper, iron
✓	B_2, folate, calcium, potassium, zinc

1 Cut the chicken on the diagonal into strips about 1 cm (½ in) thick. Heat half the oil in a wok or heavy-based frying pan. Add the chicken, onion and garlic, and cook over a moderately high heat, stirring constantly, for 2 minutes or until the chicken turns white with golden brown flecks.

2 Reduce the heat to low and add the cumin, coriander and cinnamon stick. Cook, stirring constantly, for 1 minute. Add the courgettes and stir well, then add the tomatoes with their juice and the stock. Cook for 5 minutes, stirring occasionally.

3 Meanwhile, put the couscous in a saucepan and pour over the boiling water. Add the remaining 1 tbsp oil. Stir well, cover and leave to soak, off the heat, for 5 minutes.

4 Add the sugarsnap peas and chickpeas to the chicken mixture. Cook for a further 5 minutes, stirring frequently.

5 Stir the butter into the couscous and cook over a moderate heat for 3 minutes, fluffing up with a fork to separate the grains. Pile the couscous onto a serving platter. Spoon the chicken on top and garnish with chopped coriander. Serve hot.

Another idea

● For a Middle Eastern prawn and bean couscous, use 400 g (14 oz) cooked peeled prawns (thawed if frozen), and replace the chickpeas with canned black-eyed beans. In step 1, cook the onion and garlic in the oil for 2 minutes. In step 2, omit the courgettes. In step 4, add the prawns and black-eyed beans, and instead of sugarsnap peas add 250 g (8½ oz) frozen peas, thawed, and 200 g (7 oz) green beans.

Plus points

● Couscous is low in fat and high in starchy carbohydrate. It scores low on the Glycaemic Index, which means that it breaks down slowly in the body, releasing energy gradually into the bloodstream.

● Believing chickpeas to be powerful aphrodisiacs, the Romans fed them to their stallions to improve their performance. Although this reputation seems to be long forgotten, chickpeas do contribute good amounts of soluble fibre and useful amounts of iron, folate, vitamin E and manganese to the diet.

Red mullet parcels with orange

Whole red mullet are baked in the oven on a bed of aniseed-flavoured fennel and fresh orange segments. To save time, ask your fishmonger to scale and gut the fish for you. Serve one parcel per person and accompany it with new potatoes and some simply cooked green beans.

Serves 4

2 tbsp extra virgin olive oil

2 large bulbs of fennel, halved and very thinly sliced

2 garlic cloves, chopped

8 spring onions, cut into 2.5 cm (1 in) lengths

3 small oranges

4 red mullet, about 200 g (7 oz) each, scaled and gutted, and heads removed if liked

salt and pepper

Preparation time: 15 minutes
Cooking time: 12–15 minutes

Each serving provides

kcal 270, **protein** 32 g, **fat** 12 g (of which saturated fat 1 g), **carbohydrate** 10 g (of which sugars 9 g), **fibre** 3 g

✓✓✓	B$_{12}$, C, selenium
✓✓	B$_6$, potassium
✓	B$_1$, E, folate, niacin, calcium, copper, iron

1 Preheat the oven to 220°C (425°F, gas mark 7). Heat the oil in a saucepan, add the fennel, garlic and spring onions, and cook over a moderate heat for 5 minutes or until softened.

2 Meanwhile, squeeze the juice from one of the oranges. Cut the peel and pith from the remaining 2 oranges and, holding them over the orange juice container, cut between the membrane to release the segments.

3 Divide the fennel mixture and orange segments among 4 large sheets of baking parchment. Slash each fish 3–4 times on both sides, then place on top of the vegetables and orange. Sprinkle over the orange juice, and season with salt and pepper to taste.

4 Wrap the paper round the fish and fold over to seal each parcel. Place the parcels on a baking tray and bake for 12–15 minutes or until the fish is cooked. Set the parcels on individual serving plates still sealed, so they can be opened at the table.

Some more ideas

● To make haddock parcels with vegetable spaghetti, cut 2 parsnips and 2 carrots lengthways into thin strips using a swivel vegetable peeler. Thinly slice 2 leeks lengthways to make similar-sized strips. Heat 30 g (1 oz) butter in a frying pan, add the vegetables and

1 large garlic clove, crushed, and cook for 3–4 minutes or until softened. Season to taste and pile in the centre of the parchment sheets. Place a 140 g (5 oz) piece of skinned haddock fillet (a chunky piece from the top end) on top of each one and squeeze over the juice of ¼ lemon. Dot each piece of fish with 10 g (¼ oz) butter, then wrap up the parcels. Bake for 15 minutes or until tender.

● Use 4 pieces of salmon fillet, about 140 g (5 oz) each, instead of red mullet.

Plus points

● Red mullet has lean, firm flesh that tastes almost like shellfish. It is an excellent source of selenium and provides useful amounts of potassium.

● Oranges are an excellent source of vitamin C, with 1 large orange providing around double the recommended daily amount of this vitamin. They also contain phytochemicals that are believed to help thin the blood and lower cholesterol levels, thus helping to prevent strokes and heart attacks.

Smoked fish paella

One of the reasons the so-called Mediterranean diet is considered healthy is that it features many dishes like this one from Spain, based on rice cooked in olive oil with lots of vegetables and a modest amount of protein foods. The small quantity of spicy chorizo sausage here adds an authentic Spanish flavour.

Serves 4

900 ml (1½ pints) vegetable or fish stock

large pinch of saffron threads

50 g (1¾ oz) thin chorizo sausage

400 g (14 oz) undyed smoked haddock fillet, skinned

2 tbsp extra virgin olive oil

1 large onion, finely chopped

2 large garlic cloves, crushed, or 1 tbsp bottled chopped garlic in oil, drained

250 g (8½ oz) green beans, cut into bite-sized pieces

250 g (8½ oz) paella or other short-grain rice

150 g (5½ oz) frozen peas

salt and pepper

finely chopped parsley to garnish

Preparation time: 10 minutes
Cooking time: 20 minutes

Each serving provides

kcal 465, **protein** 28 g, **fat** 13 g (of which saturated fat 1 g), **carbohydrate** 58 g (of which sugars 4 g), **fibre** 4 g

✓✓	B₁₂, folate, iron, selenium
✓	B₁, B₆, C, niacin, calcium, potassium

1 Bring the stock to the boil in a pan over a high heat. Add the saffron threads, reduce the heat and leave to simmer gently while preparing the other ingredients.

2 Remove the thick skin from the chorizo sausage and thinly slice the sausage. Cut the haddock into large chunks. Heat the olive oil in a 30 cm (12 in) round, shallow flameproof casserole, paella pan or frying pan. Add the chorizo, onion, garlic and green beans and fry for 2 minutes, stirring occasionally.

3 Add the rice and stir until all the grains are coated with oil. Add the saffron-flavoured stock and stir. Season with salt and pepper to taste. Bring to the boil, then reduce the heat to low and simmer for 3 minutes.

4 Gently stir in the haddock pieces and peas. Simmer for 20 minutes or until all the liquid has been absorbed and the rice is tender. Stir halfway through cooking, taking care not to break up the haddock too much. Sprinkle with parsley and serve.

Some more ideas

● For a smoked ham and vegetable paella, omit the haddock and chorizo sausage and instead use 300 g (10½ oz) smoked ham, cut into cubes. Instead of green beans, use 2 sliced celery sticks and 300 g (10½ oz) chopped runner beans. In step 4, stir in 1 can red kidney beans or pinto beans, about 400 g, drained and rinsed.

● Use fresh haddock fillet instead of smoked.

Plus points

● Frozen peas couldn't be quicker or easier to use, and the good news is that they are just as nutritious as fresh peas. Research comparing the level of vitamin C in fresh and frozen vegetables found that, in many cases, frozen vegetables contain higher levels of vitamin C than fresh. The longer fresh vegetables are stored, the greater the vitamin loss will be, but frozen vegetables maintain their vitamin levels throughout storage – frozen peas retain 60–70% of their vitamin C content.

● Smoked haddock, like other fish, is an excellent low-fat source of protein. It is also an excellent source of iodine, and a useful source of potassium and vitamin B₆.

Tuna and tomato pizzas

Add canned fish to a good tomato sauce, spread it on a ready-made pizza base and you have a delicious, healthy pizza in no time at all. It makes a flavourful change from the usual cheese-laden pizzas. If you don't want to use a bought pizza base, virtually any type of crusty bread can be used instead.

Serves 4

3 tsp extra virgin olive oil

1 onion, finely chopped

1 can chopped tomatoes, about 400 g

½ tsp dried oregano

good pinch of sugar

2 ready-made thick pizza bases, 230 g
(8¼ oz) each

2 tbsp tomato purée

1 can tuna in spring water, about 150 g,
drained and flaked into chunks

4 tsp capers

8 stoned black olives, sliced

salt and pepper

fresh basil leaves to garnish

Preparation time: 15 minutes
Cooking time: 10 minutes

Each serving provides

kcal 300, **protein** 28 g, **fat** 9 g (of which saturated fat 3 g), **carbohydrate** 37 g (of which sugars 9 g), **fibre** 3 g

✓✓	B_6, B_{12}, C, selenium
✓	E, niacin, copper

1 Preheat the oven to 220°C (425°F, gas mark 7). Heat 1 tsp of the oil in a small pan, add the onion and cook over a moderate heat for 4 minutes or until softened. Add the tomatoes and their juice, the oregano and sugar. Season with salt and pepper to taste. Leave the sauce to bubble for 10 minutes, stirring occasionally.

2 Put the pizza bases on 2 baking sheets. Spread 1 tbsp of tomato purée over each base. Spoon the tomato sauce over the pizzas, then add the tuna. Sprinkle with the capers and sliced olives, and drizzle the remaining 2 tsp of olive oil over the top.

3 Bake the pizzas for 10 minutes or until the bases are crisp and golden. Sprinkle with torn basil leaves and serve at once.

Some more ideas

• Use part-baked ciabatta bread, halved lengthways, as the base for the pizza. Add the topping, then bake according to the packet instructions. Alternatively, use a French stick or 4 wholemeal muffins, split in half. The muffins will provide more fibre.

• Any canned fish will work well on these pizzas. Oil-rich fish such as sardines, pilchards, anchovies, salmon and mackerel are particularly good as they are excellent sources of omega-3 essential fatty acids.

• For clam and tomato pizzas, use 1 can baby clams, about 280 g, rinsed and drained. Make the sauce by heating 1 tsp extra virgin olive oil in a pan, adding 85 g (3 oz) sliced chestnut mushrooms and frying for 3 minutes. Add 4 chopped spring onions, 1 can chopped tomatoes, about 400 g, with the juice, and 1 tsp chilli sauce. Simmer for 10 minutes to reduce the sauce, then stir in the clams, 2 tbsp chopped parsley and seasoning to taste. Spread the tomato purée over the pizza bases and spoon the clam filling on top, spreading it almost to the edges. Add 8 sliced green olives, then bake as in the main recipe.

• For a meaty pizza, cut 125 g (4½ oz) wafer-thin slices of cooked ham or turkey into fine shreds and arrange them on the tomato sauce, pushing them under the sauce a little. Sprinkle 50 g (1¾ oz) diced mozzarella cheese over the top, then bake.

Plus point

• Canned tomatoes and tomato purée are healthy storecupboard ingredients – they are both rich sources of the phytochemical lycopene (other good sources include pink grapefruit, watermelon and guava), which can help to protect against several types of cancer and heart disease.

Tofu and vegetable stir-fry

If your family is not tempted by tofu, win them round with this Chinese-style dish. The tofu is glazed with ginger and soy, and served on a bed of garlicky noodles and crisp vegetables tossed with plum sauce. Although the method may look long, the dish is incredibly quick to make and there's very little washing up!

Serves 4

250 g (8½ oz) chilled plain tofu, drained

2 tbsp soy sauce

2 tbsp tomato purée

2 tbsp sunflower oil

3 garlic cloves, crushed

2 cm (¾ in) piece fresh root ginger, peeled and finely chopped

2 sheets medium Chinese egg noodles, about 170 g (6 oz) in total

200 g (7 oz) broccoli florets, thinly sliced

200 g (7 oz) carrots, cut into matchstick strips

1 red pepper, seeded and cut into thin strips

150 ml (5 fl oz) vegetable stock or water

3 tbsp plum sauce

200 g (7 oz) pak choy, stems and leaves separated and thickly sliced

4 spring onions, cut into thin strips about 5 cm (2 in) long

1 tsp sesame seeds (optional)

Preparation time: 15 minutes
Cooking time: 11 minutes

Each serving provides ⓥ

kcal 360, protein 16 g, fat 13 g (of which saturated fat 2 g), carbohydrate 45 g (of which sugars 11 g), fibre 6 g

✓✓✓	A, C, calcium
✓✓	B₁, B₆, E, folate, copper, iron
✓	B₁₂, potassium, zinc

1 Preheat the grill. Line the grill pan with foil. Using a small knife, mark both sides of the tofu with a criss-cross pattern. Cut the tofu into quarters and place on the foil, spaced apart. Fold up the edges of the foil to make a case.

2 Mix together 1 tbsp soy sauce, 1 tbsp tomato purée, 1 tbsp oil, 1 garlic clove and the ginger, and brush the mixture on the top and base of the tofu squares. Set aside while you prepare the remaining ingredients.

3 Put the noodles in a bowl, cover with boiling water and leave to soak for 5 minutes, or according to the packet instructions.

4 Meanwhile, heat the remaining 1 tbsp oil in a wok or large frying pan. Add the broccoli and stir-fry over a high heat for 2 minutes. Add the carrots, red pepper and remaining 2 cloves of garlic, and stir-fry for 2 minutes. Stir in the stock or water and the remaining 1 tbsp soy sauce and 1 tbsp tomato purée, then mix in the plum sauce. Stir-fry for 1 minute.

5 Drain the noodles and add to the wok together with the pak choy and three-quarters of the spring onions. Stir-fry for 2 minutes or until the pak choy leaves have just wilted. Remove the wok from the heat and keep hot while you cook the tofu.

6 Put the tofu under the grill and cook for 2 minutes. Turn it over and grill the other side for 1 minute. Sprinkle the sesame seeds over and cook for a further 1 minute.

7 Spoon the vegetables and noodles into bowls, place a piece of tofu in the centre of each and garnish with the remaining spring onions. Serve hot.

Plus points

● Tofu is high in protein – pressed tofu contains 15.8% and plain 11.5% – but low in saturated fat. It is also rich in iron and B vitamins and is a useful source of calcium – just 50 g (1¾ oz) provides about 40% of the recommended daily amount of calcium for an adult woman. As the fibre from the soya bean is removed during processing, tofu is very easy to digest.

● Evidence from around the world is accumulating to suggest that eating soya beans and products made from soya beans, such as tofu, may help to reduce the risk of certain cancers, heart disease and osteoporosis as well as reducing symptoms associated with the menopause.

family meals in minutes

Some more ideas

• For a chicken and green vegetable stir-fry, use 4 skinless boneless chicken breasts (fillets), about 140 g (5 oz) each. Spread the skinned side with the soy and ginger glaze, then grill for 6 minutes on each side. Meanwhile, make the stir-fry, substituting courgettes for the carrots, and a green pepper in place of the red; omit the noodles. Turn the chicken glazed side uppermost and sprinkle with 2 tsp sesame seeds. Grill for 2 more minutes or until lightly browned. Serve the chicken on the vegetables, with plain boiled rice to accompany.

• Instead of plum sauce, use 3 tbsp yellow bean paste or 2 tbsp hoisin sauce. Other flavouring ideas are to replace 2–3 tbsp of the stock with dry sherry, or up to 100 ml (3½ fl oz) stock with white wine.

• Fresh plain tofu, which is the most widely available, is found in the chiller cabinet of most supermarkets. It is suspended in water, so needs to be well drained before use. Firm pressed tofu, which is usually sold in long-life cartons, is equally good for this dish as it holds its shape well. It doesn't absorb flavours as readily, so it is a good idea to marinate it in the soy sauce mixture for 10–15 minutes (or as long as possible) before grilling.

• If pak choy is unavailable, you can use Swiss chard or spinach instead.

Penne with artichokes and olives

This light pasta dish is ideal for summer suppers as only the pasta needs to be cooked. Once al dente, it is simply tossed, still warm, with diced tomatoes, quartered artichoke hearts, black olives and a rich lemony dressing flavoured with sun-dried tomato paste and garlic.

Serves 4

400 g (14 oz) penne or other pasta shapes

500 g (1 lb 2 oz) ripe plum tomatoes, diced

4 spring onions, finely chopped

170 g (6 oz) artichoke hearts from a can or jar, drained and quartered

55 g (2 oz) stoned black olives

4 heaped tbsp Parmesan cheese shavings to garnish

Tomato and oregano dressing

3 tbsp extra virgin olive oil or oil from the jar of artichokes

grated zest and juice of 1 lemon

2 tbsp sun-dried tomato paste

2 garlic cloves, crushed

6 tbsp chopped fresh oregano

salt and pepper

Preparation and cooking time: 20–25 minutes

Each serving provides

Ⓥ

kcal 550, protein 20 g, fat 17 g (of which saturated fat 5 g), carbohydrate 83 g (of which sugars 8 g), fibre 5 g

✓✓	A, C, calcium, iron
✓	B₁, B₆, E, folate, potassium, selenium, zinc

1 Cook the pasta in a large saucepan of boiling water for 10–12 minutes, or according to the packet instructions, until just al dente.

2 Meanwhile, mix together the tomatoes, spring onions, artichoke hearts and olives in a large serving bowl. In a separate small bowl, mix the oil with the lemon zest and juice, tomato paste, garlic, oregano, and salt and pepper to taste.

3 Drain the pasta and add to the large serving bowl. Drizzle over the dressing and toss well. Garnish with shavings of Parmesan (a swivel vegetable peeler is good for making these) and serve immediately while the pasta is still warm.

Some more ideas

● Vary the herbs: fresh basil is also delicious, as is flat-leaf parsley, or parsley mixed with other herbs such as a little finely chopped rosemary or sage.

● If you haven't any fresh herbs, add 1 tbsp pesto instead.

● For a mellower dressing, replace the lemon juice with 4 tsp balsamic vinegar.

● For a Sicilian-inspired pasta salad, omit the artichokes and use 85 g (3 oz) stoned black olives, 8 canned anchovy fillets, about 30 g (1 oz) in total, and 2 tbsp drained capers. Omit the sun-dried tomato paste from the dressing, and replace the oregano with 6 tbsp chopped fresh tarragon or flat-leaf parsley.

● For a more traditional, softer pasta sauce, simmer the tomatoes, spring onions, artichoke hearts and olives in a saucepan for 5 minutes, then mix with the dressing ingredients.

● Instead of Parmesan, top the salad with crumbled feta cheese, diced brie or grated Lancashire or Cheshire cheese.

● Leftover pasta salad makes a good packed lunch the next day. Transfer to a well-sealed plastic container and pack in a cool bag with a mini frozen ice pack.

Plus points

● Pasta is a healthy low-fat food – it's the rich buttery sauces that pile on the calories and fat. Opting for olive oil instead of butter, or, better still, using small amounts of oil in vegetable sauces, is the best way to keep saturated fat to a minimum.

● Adding fresh lemon juice to the dressing boosts the levels of vitamin C in this dish.

Caribbean butternut squash and sweetcorn stew

Butternut squash has a lovely firm texture, ideal for cooking in stews. Combined with black-eyed beans, sweetcorn and red pepper it makes a nutritious family supper dish that is perfect for cold winter days. Serve with boiled rice or warm crusty bread.

Serves 4

1 tbsp extra virgin olive oil

1 onion, sliced

2 garlic cloves, crushed

1 butternut squash, about 675 g (1½ lb), peeled and cut into 1 cm (½ in) cubes

1 red pepper, seeded and sliced

1 bay leaf

1 can chopped tomatoes, about 400 g

1 can black-eyed beans, about 410 g, drained and rinsed

1 can sweetcorn kernels, about 200 g, drained

300 ml (10 fl oz) vegetable stock

1 tbsp Worcestershire sauce, or to taste

1 tsp Tabasco sauce, or to taste

1 tbsp dark muscovado sugar

1–2 tsp balsamic vinegar

chopped parsley to garnish

Preparation and cooking time: 30 minutes

Each serving provides

kcal 335, **protein** 15 g, **fat** 4 g (of which saturated fat 1 g), **carbohydrate** 62 g (of which sugars 21 g), **fibre** 9 g

✓✓✓	A, B$_6$, C, folate
✓✓	B$_1$, E, copper, iron, potassium
✓	calcium, zinc

1 Heat the oil in a large saucepan and add the onion, garlic, butternut squash, red pepper and bay leaf. Stir well, then cover the pan and allow the vegetables to sweat for 5 minutes, stirring occasionally.

2 Add the tomatoes with their juice, the black-eyed beans and sweetcorn, and stir to mix. Add the stock, Worcestershire sauce, Tabasco sauce, sugar and vinegar and stir again. Cover and simmer for 15 minutes or until the squash is tender.

3 Sprinkle the parsley over the stew and serve at once.

Some more ideas

• Give the stew an Indian flavour. Soften the sliced onion and garlic in the olive oil for 2–3 minutes, then stir in 2 tbsp medium balti paste. Add the butternut squash with 150 g (5½ oz) thickly sliced baby corn. Cover and cook for 5–6 minutes. Replace the black-eyed beans with borlotti beans, adding them with the canned tomatoes and stock (omit the sweetcorn kernels). Garnish with 2 tbsp chopped fresh coriander instead of parsley, and serve with boiled jasmine rice or warm naan bread.

• For a vegetarian alternative, use mushroom ketchup instead of Worcestershire sauce.

Plus points

• There are over 25 species of pumpkin and squash, some of which have been cultivated for 9000 years. All varieties are rich in beta-carotene and contain useful amounts of vitamin C.

• If you have the time, leave the freshly crushed garlic cloves to stand for 10 minutes or so before starting to cook. Researchers at Penn State University in the USA have found that this maximises the formation and retention of cancer-fighting compounds.

Spinach and potato frittata

This flat omelette makes a delicious vegetarian main course, and can be eaten hot or at room temperature. It is a very versatile recipe, as almost anything can be added to it – a handy way of using up leftovers. Serve with toasted ciabatta bread and sliced tomatoes and/or a mixed green salad for a quick supper.

Serves 4

500 g (1 lb 2 oz) potatoes, scrubbed and cut into 1 cm (½ in) cubes

225 g (8 oz) baby spinach leaves, trimmed of any large stalks

1 tbsp extra virgin olive oil

1 red pepper, quartered lengthways, seeded and thinly sliced

5–6 spring onions, thinly sliced

5 eggs

3 tbsp freshly grated Parmesan cheese

salt and pepper

Preparation and cooking time: 30 minutes

Each serving provides ⓥ

kcal 320, **protein** 19 g, **fat** 15 g (of which saturated fat 5 g), **carbohydrate** 26 g (of which sugars 6 g), **fibre** 4 g

✓✓✓	A, B$_6$, B$_{12}$, C
✓✓	folate, calcium, iron
✓	B$_1$, B$_2$, E, potassium, zinc

1 Cook the potatoes in a saucepan of boiling water for 5–6 minutes or until almost tender. Put the spinach in a steamer or colander over the potatoes and cook for another 5 minutes or until the potatoes are tender and the spinach has wilted. Drain the potatoes. Press the spinach with the back of a spoon to extract excess moisture, then chop.

2 Heat the oil in a non-stick frying pan that is about 25 cm (10 in) in diameter. Add the pepper slices and sauté over a moderate heat for 2 minutes. Stir in the potatoes and spring onions and continue cooking for 2 minutes.

3 Beat the eggs in a large bowl, season with salt and pepper and mix in the spinach. With a draining spoon, remove about half of the vegetables from the pan and add to the egg mixture, leaving the oil in the pan. Stir the egg and vegetables briefly to mix, then pour into the frying pan. Cover and cook, without stirring, for about 6 minutes or until the omelette is almost set but still a little soft on top. Meanwhile, preheat the grill.

4 Dust the top of the frittata with the Parmesan cheese and place under the grill. Cook for 3–4 minutes or until browned and puffed around the edges. Cut into quarters or wedges and serve.

Plus points

● Spinach is a good source of several antioxidants, including vitamin C and vitamin E, and it provides useful amounts of folate, niacin and B$_6$. Contrary to popular belief, it is not a particularly good source of iron.

● Although in the past people with a high risk of heart disease or stroke were advised to restrict the number of eggs they ate to 2 a week, a recent study suggests that unless you suffer from diabetes you can safely eat up to one egg a day.

Some more ideas

● For a courgette and potato frittata, replace the spinach with 1 large or 2 small courgettes, quartered lengthways and sliced, and use 1 thinly sliced small leek instead of spring onions. Sauté the leek and courgette with the pepper slices for 3–4 minutes. Add the potatoes and stir. Mix a handful of torn fresh basil leaves with the beaten eggs, and cook the omelette as in the main recipe.

● Make a smoked salmon frittata. Omit the potatoes and red pepper, and sauté a courgette, quartered lengthways and sliced, with the spring onions. Add 75 g (2½ oz) slivered smoked salmon to the eggs with the spinach. Finish the frittata under the grill without the Parmesan.

family meals in minutes

Bulghur wheat pilaf

The combination of grains and beans is common to all cuisines with a tradition of vegetarian meals. In this delicious one-pot main dish, ground coriander and cinnamon and dried apricots add a Middle Eastern flavour.

Serves 4

2 eggs

2 tbsp sunflower oil

1 large onion, finely chopped

2 large garlic cloves, crushed

1½ tsp ground coriander

1 tsp ground cinnamon

1 tsp turmeric

pinch of crushed dried chillies (optional)

1 can butter beans, about 400 g, drained and rinsed

100 g (3½ oz) ready-to-eat dried apricots

300 g (10½ oz) bulghur wheat

150 g (5½ oz) thin green beans, halved

salt and pepper

fresh coriander leaves to garnish

Preparation and cooking time: 30 minutes

Each serving provides

kcal 485, **protein** 18 g, **fat** 11 g (of which saturated fat 2 g), **carbohydrate** 81 g (of which sugars 13 g), **fibre** 7 g

✓✓ E, copper, iron

✓ A, B₁, B₂, B₁₂, folate, calcium, potassium

1 Place the eggs in a saucepan of cold water, bring to the boil and boil gently for 10 minutes. Drain the eggs and cool under cold running water. Set aside.

2 While the eggs are cooking, heat the oil in a large flameproof casserole. Add the onion and garlic and fry for 3 minutes, stirring occasionally. Stir in the ground coriander, cinnamon, turmeric and chillies, if using. Stir for a further minute.

3 Add the butter beans and apricots, and stir to coat them with the spices. Stir in the bulghur wheat and green beans, then pour in enough water to cover by about 2 cm (¾ in). Season with salt and pepper to taste. Bring to the boil, then reduce the heat to its lowest setting. Cover and simmer for 20 minutes or until all the liquid has been absorbed.

4 While the stew is cooking, shell and slice the eggs. Fluff the bulghur wheat with a fork and adjust the seasoning, if necessary. Serve hot, garnished with the egg slices and sprinkled with coriander leaves.

Plus points

● Bulghur wheat is a good low-fat source of starchy (complex) carbohydrate. It contains useful amounts of some of the B vitamins, particularly B₁, as well as copper and iron.

● Ready-to-eat dried apricots are a versatile and nutritious ingredient and it is well worth keeping a packet in your storecupboard. They are ideal for quick snacks, and they can be added to breakfast cereals, baked goods, stews and casseroles. They provide beta-carotene, which is converted into vitamin A in the body, and are a useful source of iron, calcium and fibre.

Another idea

● Couscous, like bulghur wheat, is a great low-fat source of starchy carbohydrate. To make a couscous pilaf, fry 1 large diced red pepper with the onion and garlic. Instead of green beans, use 140 g (5 oz) carrots, chopped, adding them with the spices. In step 3, stir in 200 g (7 oz) couscous, 100 g (3½ oz) raisins, or a mixture of raisins and sultanas, and a can of chickpeas, about 400 g, drained. Add enough water to cover the ingredients by about 1 cm (½ in) and simmer, covered, for 15 minutes. Fluff the couscous with a fork, adjust the seasoning and stir in 200 g (7 oz) baby spinach leaves. Sprinkle with chopped parsley or fresh coriander and serve.

family meals in minutes

Chicken and pinto bean tacos

Here, tender chicken in a spicy mixture is quickly cooked to make a succulent filling for crisp taco shells. Sliced peppers and pinto or borlotti beans add to the mix, as does a scattering of shredded lettuce, spring onions and avocado. A dash of Tabasco sauce or other bottled hot sauce gives a piquant kick.

Serves 4

350 g (12½ oz) skinless boneless chicken breasts (fillets), cut into strips

3 garlic cloves, chopped

juice of 1 lime

¾–1 tsp Mexican seasoning mix

1 tbsp extra virgin olive oil

2 red, green or yellow peppers, seeded and thinly sliced

1 can pinto or borlotti beans, about 400 g, drained and rinsed

8 taco shells (crisp corn tortilla shells)

1 avocado

85 g (3 oz) crisp lettuce leaves, torn or shredded

3 spring onions, thinly sliced

3 tbsp fresh coriander leaves

1 tomato, diced or sliced

Tabasco or other hot sauce to taste

4 tbsp fromage frais

salt and pepper

Preparation and cooking time: 25 minutes

Each serving provides

kcal 490, protein 32 g, fat 21 g (of which saturated fat 3 g), carbohydrate 45 g (of which sugars 4 g), fibre 3 g

✓✓✓	C, B$_6$
✓✓	B$_1$, E, folate, niacin, copper, iron, zinc
✓	A, B$_2$, selenium

1 Preheat the oven to 180°C (350°F, gas mark 4). Put the chicken, garlic, lime juice and Mexican seasoning mix in a bowl and season to taste with salt and pepper. Mix well.

2 Heat the oil in a heavy non-stick frying pan or wok. Add the chicken mixture and cook for 1 minute without stirring. Add the peppers and stir-fry over a high heat for 3–5 minutes or until the chicken is lightly browned. Add the beans and heat them through, stirring occasionally.

3 Meanwhile, arrange the taco shells, open end down, on a baking tray and warm in the oven for 2–3 minutes. Peel and dice the avocado.

4 Spoon the chicken and pepper mixture into the taco shells, dividing it equally among them. Add the avocado, lettuce, spring onions, tomato, coriander and Tabasco or other hot sauce to taste. Serve at once, with the fromage frais to be spooned on top of the tacos.

Some more ideas

• Use 1 red or green pepper and replace the other pepper with 150 g (5½ oz) baby corn or sweetcorn kernels (frozen or canned). Add to the pan with the chicken mixture.

• For lamb and hummus wraps, trim any fat from 250 g (8½ oz) lean boneless lamb, such as leg, and slice thinly. Heat 1 tbsp extra virgin olive oil in a frying pan, add the lamb with 1 red pepper, seeded and cut into thin strips, 3 chopped garlic cloves, the juice of 1 lemon, ½ tsp ground cumin, and salt and pepper to taste, and fry for 7–10 minutes. Meanwhile, heat 4 large plain or tomato-flavoured flour tortillas in the oven or microwave, according to the packet instructions. Spread each tortilla with about 45 g (1½ oz) hummus, top with a portion of the lamb mixture and add some sliced or diced cucumber, sliced or diced tomatoes and chopped fresh mint and coriander. Sprinkle with 2–3 chopped spring onions and a little Tabasco or other hot sauce, if desired, then roll up. Serve hot.

Plus points

• Avocados are a rich source of monounsaturated fat and vitamin B$_6$ – one small avocado provides over half the daily requirement for B$_6$. They also contribute useful amounts of vitamin E and several important phytochemicals.

• Herbs, spices and mixtures such as the Mexican seasoning used in this recipe are a good way of adding flavour to food rather than using lots of salt

Curried lentil and vegetable pilaf

Curries usually take a long time to prepare and cook, but by using some supermarket convenience foods, such as ready-prepared vegetables, and ginger and garlic bottled in oil, this dish can be on the table in half an hour. It makes a one-dish vegetarian meal that is rich in protein, starchy carbohydrate and other essential nutrients.

Serves 4

100 g (3½ oz) creamed coconut
900 ml (1½ pints) vegetable stock or water
2 tbsp sunflower oil
1½ tsp cumin seeds
2 tsp ground coriander
1 tsp bottled chopped root ginger in oil, drained
1 tsp bottled chopped garlic in oil, drained
½ tsp cayenne pepper, or to taste
200 g (7 oz) basmati rice, rinsed
200 g (7 oz) red lentils
500 g (1 lb 2 oz) prepared mixed vegetables, such as carrots, beans, broccoli and cauliflower
salt and pepper
chopped fresh coriander or parsley to garnish

To serve
2 bananas
finely grated zest of 1 lime
lime juice to taste

Preparation and cooking time: about 30 minutes

Each serving provides

kcal 560, **protein** 20 g, **fat** 16 g (of which saturated fat 9 g), **carbohydrate** 87 g (of which sugars 18 g), **fibre** 5 g

✓✓✓	A
✓✓	B₁, B₆, C, folate, copper, iron
✓	calcium, potassium, zinc

1 Grate the creamed coconut into a saucepan and add the stock. Bring to a simmer over a moderate heat, stirring occasionally until the coconut has melted.

2 Meanwhile, heat the oil in a large flameproof casserole or frying pan with a lid. Add the cumin seeds and stir-fry over a moderately high heat until they begin to sizzle and give off their aroma. Stir in the ground coriander, ginger, garlic and cayenne pepper and stir-fry for about 1 minute.

3 Stir in the rice, lentils and vegetables. Pour in the coconut stock and stir to mix everything together. Bring to the boil, then reduce the heat to low, cover and simmer for 20 minutes, without removing the lid, until the rice and lentils are tender and all the liquid has been absorbed.

4 Just before the pilaf finishes cooking, slice the bananas into a bowl. Add the lime zest and sprinkle over lime juice to taste.

5 When the pilaf is ready, adjust the seasoning if necessary, and fluff up the rice with a fork. Sprinkle with the chopped coriander or parsley and serve at once, with the bananas.

Some more ideas

• Use 500 g (1 lb 2 oz) mixed frozen vegetables, thawed, adding them 5 minutes before the end of the cooking time.

• Make a spice paste. Put 1½ tsp each cumin and coriander seeds in a mortar and ½ tsp bottled chopped root ginger in oil, drained, and grind to a paste. Heat the oil, add the spice paste and 1 tsp turmeric, and stir-fry for 1 minute.

• Instead of the lime-flavoured banana chutney, mix 250 g (8½ oz) plain low-fat yogurt with ¼ cucumber, finely chopped, and season with a pinch each of ground cumin, coriander and cayenne pepper.

• To reduce the fat, omit the creamed coconut and use plain vegetable stock.

Plus points

• The fresh banana chutney makes a good alternative to traditional mango chutney, which is high in sugar. The addition of lime juice helps to boost the vitamin C content and this, in turn, enhances the absorption of iron from the lentils.

• Creamed coconut is very high in saturated fat, but like other high-fat foods it can still be included in a healthy diet if eaten in moderation.

Fast Food for Friends

Nutritious and easy dishes for entertaining

You don't need to spend hours in the kitchen when having friends round. Here are lots of fast, healthy recipes for entertaining at home without stress. Fish is a perfect choice – steamed sea bass with spring vegetables and couscous, or Thai-style crab cakes with a sweet and sour dipping sauce are sure to impress your guests. Pork medallions seared on a ridged cast-iron grill pan and finished with honey and kumquats is another quick and easy option, or try griddled aubergine slices and goat's cheese with ribbon noodles and tomato sauce.

Mixed seafood and noodle broth

In China soups are not served at the beginning of the meal but in between courses or dishes. This is why they are made with a light stock, so they are more appropriate as a starter in a Western meal. You can part-prepare this soup ahead, then add the scallops, vegetables and noodles just before serving.

Serves 6

55 g (2 oz) fine stir-fry rice noodles, broken into 10 cm (4 in) lengths

2 tsp groundnut oil

2.5 cm (1 in) piece fresh root ginger, finely chopped

75 g (2½ oz) shiitake mushrooms, stalks discarded and caps thinly sliced

1.2 litres (2 pints) chicken stock

1 tbsp dry sherry

2 tbsp light soy sauce

125 g (4½ oz) cooked mixed seafood, such as prawns, squid and queen scallops

75 g (2½ oz) Chinese leaves, shredded

4 spring onions, thinly sliced

75 g (2½ oz) beansprouts

fresh coriander leaves to garnish

chilli sauce to serve

Preparation and cooking time: 25 minutes

1 Put the noodles in a bowl and pour over plenty of boiling water. Set aside to soak for 4 minutes.

2 Meanwhile, heat the groundnut oil in a large saucepan, add the ginger and mushrooms, and cook for about 2 minutes to soften slightly. Add the stock, sherry and soy sauce, and bring to the boil.

3 Halve the scallops if they are large. Add the mixed seafood to the boiling stock together with the Chinese leaves, spring onions and beansprouts. Bring back to the boil and cook for 1 minute or until the seafood is heated through.

4 Drain the noodles and add to the soup. Bring back to the boil, then ladle into large soup bowls. Scatter over a few fresh coriander leaves and serve with chilli sauce, to be added to taste.

Another idea

● For a crab and noodle broth, use 1 can white crab meat, about 170 g, drained, instead of the mixed seafood. Replace the mushrooms with 100 g (3½ oz) thinly sliced baby corn and 100 g (3½ oz) diced courgettes, cooking them with the ginger for 1 minute. In step 3, omit the Chinese leaves. After adding the rice noodles in step 4, bring to the boil and season with 1 tbsp fish sauce.

Plus points

● Seafood provides an excellent source of low-fat protein and a range of other nutrients. Scallops are an excellent source of selenium and B_{12}, and a useful source of phosphorus and potassium. Prawns provide calcium, while squid is an excellent source of B_{12}.

● Shiitake mushrooms contain the B vitamins B_2, niacin and pantothenic acid. They also provide potassium and good quantities of copper.

● Rice noodles are gluten-free and wheat-free, making them useful for people with gluten intolerances or wheat allergies.

Each serving provides

kcal 80, **protein** 5 g, **fat** 1.5 g (of which saturated fat 0.3 g), **carbohydrate** 9 g (of which sugars 1 g), **fibre** 0.5 g

✓✓	B_{12}
✓	copper, selenium

Lamb steaks with rosemary

Quick-cooking lamb steaks are coated with a rich-flavoured sauce made with red onions, garlic, fresh rosemary and black olives, and accompanied by a high-fibre, garlicky flageolet bean mash. Serve with lots of crusty bread and a green vegetable such as grilled courgettes or pan-wilted fresh spinach.

Serves 4

2 tbsp extra virgin olive oil

2 large red onions, thinly sliced

3 large garlic cloves, thinly shredded

6 sprigs of fresh rosemary, each about 2.5 cm (1 in) long, plus extra sprigs to garnish

4 lean lamb steaks, about 130 g (4¾ oz) each

1 tbsp balsamic vinegar

4 tbsp red wine

30 g (1 oz) stoned black olives, sliced

1 tsp sugar

200 ml (7 fl oz) vegetable stock

Flageolet bean and garlic mash

1 tbsp extra virgin olive oil

3 garlic cloves

2 cans flageolet beans, about 400 g each, drained and rinsed

5 tbsp vegetable stock

3 tbsp chopped parsley

salt and pepper

Preparation and cooking time: 30 minutes

Each serving provides

kcal 500, protein 40 g, fat 21 g (of which saturated fat 6 g), carbohydrate 38 g (of which sugars 12 g), fibre 12 g

✓✓✓	B₁₂, iron, zinc
✓✓	D₁, C, niacin, calcium
✓	A, B₂, E, copper, potassium, selenium

1 Heat the olive oil in a large frying pan, add the onions, garlic and rosemary, and cook over a moderate heat for about 10 minutes, stirring frequently, until the onions have softened and are starting to turn golden.

2 Meanwhile, make the flageolet bean and garlic mash. Heat the olive oil in a saucepan, add the peeled garlic cloves and cook over a very low heat for 4–5 minutes or until tender. Add the flageolet beans and vegetable stock, cover the pan and cook gently for 4–5 minutes to heat through. Mash until smooth, season to taste and stir in the parsley. Keep warm.

3 Push the onions to the side of the frying pan, and add the lamb steaks. Fry for 3–4 minutes on each side, depending on how well done you like your meat.

4 Lift the lamb steaks from the pan and place on warmed serving plates. Add the balsamic vinegar, wine, olives and sugar to the frying pan and cook over a high heat until the liquid has evaporated. Stir in the stock and bubble for 1 more minute, then pour the sauce over the lamb. Garnish with fresh sprigs of rosemary and serve with the flageolet bean mash.

Some more ideas

● This is delicious with grilled courgettes. Halve the courgettes lengthways, then brush the cut side with extra virgin olive oil and season to taste (flavour the oil with a little garlic, if liked). Grill, cut side up, for 10 minutes or until the courgettes are tender and golden.

● Use 2 tbsp shredded fresh basil instead of parsley in the mash.

● To make Italian-style pork chops with olives, sear 4 boneless pork loin chops with 2 sliced garlic cloves in 1 tbsp extra virgin olive oil for 3–4 minutes on each side. Lift the meat from the pan and keep warm. Add 4 large tomatoes, chopped, to the pan with 6 anchovy fillets, chopped, 2 tbsp extra dry white vermouth, 100 ml (3½ fl oz) vegetable stock, 30 g (1 oz) sliced black olives and ½ vegetable stock cube. Bring to the boil, stirring, and simmer for 5 minutes to make a sauce for the chops.

Plus points

● Red onions have been shown to contain higher levels of flavonoids (compounds that can help to protect against heart disease) than white onions.

● Parsley is a good source of vitamin C, and is rich in beta-carotene and potassium.

Thai-style crab cakes

Made from crab meat and white fish, with all the classic flavouring ingredients of Thai cooking, these cakes taste sensational, and they come with a dipping sauce and crunchy salad. Serve with Thai fragrant rice.

Serves 4

2 cans white meat crab, about 170 g each, drained and patted dry with kitchen paper

225 g (8 oz) skinless white fish fillets, such as cod or haddock, cut into chunks

1 tbsp Thai red curry paste

1 fresh lime leaf

2 tbsp chopped fresh coriander

½ tsp caster sugar

1 egg, beaten

2 carrots, finely chopped

½ cucumber, finely chopped

4 spring onions, finely chopped

2 tbsp groundnut or sunflower oil for frying

salt

Sweet and sour dipping sauce

3 tbsp white wine or cider vinegar

50 g (1¾ oz) caster sugar

1 tbsp fish sauce

1 fresh red chilli, seeded and finely chopped

To garnish

lime wedges

sprigs of fresh coriander

Preparation and cooking time: 30 minutes

Each serving provides

kcal 330, **protein** 30 g, **fat** 13 g (of which saturated fat 2 g), **carbohydrate** 23 g (of which sugars 22 g), **fibre** 2 g

✓✓✓	A, copper
✓✓	B$_6$, B$_{12}$, E, selenium, zinc
✓	B$_1$, folate, calcium, potassium

1 Place the crab and white fish in a food processor or blender and process until mixed. Add the red curry paste, lime leaf, chopped coriander, sugar, a pinch of salt and the egg. Process again to mix. Divide the mixture into 12 even-sized pieces. Roll each one into a ball, then flatten to make a small cake. Chill while making the dipping sauce.

2 Gently heat the vinegar, sugar, fish sauce and 2 tbsp water in a small pan until the sugar dissolves. Boil for 2–3 minutes or until syrupy, then remove from the heat and allow to cool before adding the chilli.

3 Mix together the carrots, cucumber and spring onions in a serving bowl or in 4 small individual dishes.

4 Heat the oil in a large non-stick frying pan. Fry the crab cakes for 2–3 minutes on each side or until golden and cooked through. Drain on kitchen paper. Serve garnished with lime wedges and sprigs of coriander, with the dipping sauce and the carrot and cucumber salad.

Some more ideas

● If you like a really hot dipping sauce, include the chilli seeds. Some chopped peanuts could also be added to the sauce.

● Halve the quantities of carrot, cucumber and spring onion, and add to the dipping sauce.

● For Thai-style prawn cakes, use 225 g (8 oz) peeled cooked prawns instead of the crab. Or make fish cakes using all white fish fillet – 450 g (1 lb) in total.

● Try Thai green curry paste instead of red – it is slightly milder and more aromatic.

● If you can't find lime leaves, use the grated zest of 1 lime instead.

Plus points

● Crab meat is an excellent low-fat source of protein and is a good source of phosphorus, which is important for healthy bones and teeth.

● Results from a study that compared the diets of over 5500 people in Holland, showed that those people who ate fish regularly were less likely to develop dementia in later life.

● Some studies suggest that eating chillies can help to protect against gastric ulcers. Chillies cause the stomach lining to secrete a mucus that coats the stomach, protecting it from damage by irritants such as aspirin or alcohol.

Salmon with mango salsa

Here is a wonderful mixture of bright colours and zingy flavours, from the peppery topping on the salmon to the mustardy watercress and fragrant mango salsa with its surprise kick. This is certainly vitality food – it looks great, is fun to eat and is bursting with vitamins and minerals.

Serves 4

4 pieces of salmon fillet, 150 g (5½ oz) each

4 tsp mixed peppercorns (black, white, green and pink)

675 g (1½ lb) baby new potatoes, scrubbed, and halved if large

170 g (6 oz) watercress

Mango salsa

1 mango, about 400 g (14 oz)

3 spring onions, finely chopped

1–2 tsp pink peppercorns in brine, rinsed and roughly chopped

3 tbsp chopped fresh coriander

2 tbsp lime juice

2 tbsp extra virgin olive oil

Tabasco sauce to taste

Preparation and cooking time: 30 minutes

Each serving provides

kcal 500, **protein** 32 g, **fat** 24 g (of which saturated fat 5 g), **carbohydrate** 41 g (of which sugars 16 g), **fibre** 5 g

✓✓✓	A, B$_6$, B$_{12}$
✓✓	B$_1$, niacin, copper, iron, potassium, selenium
✓	B$_2$, E, folate, zinc

1 Check the salmon fillets for any tiny pin bones and remove them with tweezers. Roughly crush the peppercorns in a pestle and mortar. Press them into the flesh side of the salmon. Set aside.

2 Put the potatoes in a saucepan, cover with boiling water and bring back to the boil. Reduce the heat and simmer for 10–12 minutes or until tender. At the same time, preheat a ridged cast-iron grill pan.

3 Meanwhile, make the salsa. Stone and peel the mango, and dice the flesh. Put into a large bowl and mix in the spring onions, pink peppercorns, coriander, lime juice, olive oil and a good dash of Tabasco sauce.

4 Brush the grill pan with a little oil if necessary, then put the salmon fillets in, skin side down. Cook over a moderately high heat for 4 minutes. Turn them over and cook for another 4 minutes or until the fish is cooked. Drain the potatoes.

5 Arrange the watercress and new potatoes on 4 serving plates. Place the salmon on top and serve with the mango salsa.

Some more ideas

● Instead of chopping the pink peppercorns, leave them whole in the mango salsa.

● The mango salsa is delicious with other oily fish, such as tuna, swordfish and mackerel.

● Top the salmon fillets with a horseradish crust instead of the peppercorns. Mix 2 tbsp creamed horseradish with 1 egg yolk and dip in the fish fillets, flesh side only. Mix 85 g (3 oz) fresh breadcrumbs with 1 tbsp chopped parsley and press the mixture onto the horseradish-coated fish. Heat 15 g (½ oz) butter and 1 tsp sunflower oil in a frying pan. Add the salmon, crust side down, and cook for 2 minutes. Turn the fish over and cook for a further 4–5 minutes. Serve on the potatoes and a mixture of cherry tomatoes and salad leaves, such as rocket and mizuna (a spiky, green Japanese salad leaf).

Plus point

● Salmon is rich in omega-3 fatty acids, a type of polyunsaturated fat thought to help protect against coronary heart disease and strokes by making blood less 'sticky' and therefore less likely to clot. A diet rich in omega-3 fatty acids may also be helpful in preventing and treating arthritis. Salmon is also an excellent source of vitamins B$_6$ and B$_{12}$, and provides selenium and potassium.

fast food for friends

Poached skate with vegetables

Skate wings have a fine texture and flavour as well as an intriguing shape. Poaching them in stock with lots of vegetables is simple and quick, and lets each ingredient add its flavour to the others. A ladleful of the poaching stock turns sautéed peppers and tomatoes into a sauce to serve with the fish and vegetables.

Serves 4

600 ml (1 pint) chicken or fish stock

675 g (1½ lb) new potatoes, scrubbed and sliced

3 spring onions, thinly sliced

2–3 sprigs of fresh thyme

2 garlic cloves, chopped

4 medium or 2 large skate wings, 750 g (1 lb 10 oz) in total

2 courgettes, thinly sliced

juice of ½ lemon

2 tbsp extra virgin olive oil

1 red pepper, seeded and diced

1 green pepper, seeded and diced

3–4 large ripe tomatoes, diced

6 black olives, stoned and halved

6 green olives, stoned and halved

salt and pepper

chopped fresh herbs to garnish

lemon wedges to serve

Preparation and cooking time: 30 minutes

Each serving provides

kcal 350, **protein** 34 g, **fat** 9 g (of which saturated fat 1 g), **carbohydrate** 37 g (of which sugars 12 g), **fibre** 5 g

✓✓✓	A, B$_6$, B$_{12}$, C
✓✓	B$_1$, potassium
✓	B$_2$, E, folate, niacin, calcium, copper, zinc

1 Bring the stock to the boil in a large shallow saucepan. Add the potatoes and enough boiling water to cover them. Add the spring onions, thyme and half of the garlic. Bring back to the boil, then reduce the heat to moderate and cover. Simmer for about 5 minutes or until the potatoes are almost tender.

2 Add the skate wings to the pan and lay the courgette slices on top. Sprinkle over the lemon juice. The potatoes should be submerged in liquid, so add more boiling water if necessary. Cover again and cook over a moderately high heat for 5–7 minutes or until the potatoes are tender and the skate will flake when tested with a fork.

3 Meanwhile, heat 1½ tbsp of the olive oil in a frying pan and add the remaining garlic and the red and green peppers. Cook for 3–4 minutes or until the vegetables have softened. Add the tomatoes and cook over a high heat for 1–2 minutes, stirring.

4 Add a ladleful – about 120 ml (4 fl oz) – of the fish poaching liquid to the tomato mixture, and bubble over a high heat for 6–7 minutes or until the liquid has almost all evaporated. Add the olives and season with salt and pepper to taste. Remove the sauce from the heat and keep warm.

5 Lift the fish and vegetables from the pan with a draining spoon or fish slice and place on individual serving plates. Spoon the sauce over the fish. Garnish with chopped herbs and drizzle over the remaining ½ tbsp of olive oil. Serve with lemon wedges.

Another idea

• For saffron-scented fish with green beans, use 500 g (1 lb 2 oz) of skinless cod, haddock or monkfish fillet, cut into 4 pieces. Add 1 large pinch of saffron threads to the stock in step 1. In step 2, add the fish, which will need 7–10 minutes cooking. Instead of courgettes, use 250 g (8½ oz) fine green beans, adding them 3–4 minutes before the end of cooking.

Plus points

• Skate is an excellent source of vitamin B$_{12}$ and a useful source of potassium, vitamins B$_1$ and B$_6$ and niacin.

• Many people assume that olives are high in calories, but in fact both the black and green varieties provide relatively few – 30 g (1 oz) olives, which is about 10, contain about 30 kcals and just 3 g fat. Olives are a source of vitamin E, but are usually not eaten in large enough quantities to make a significant contribution to the diet.

Calf's liver with sherry sauce

Calf's liver is more expensive than other livers, but has the finest, most delicate flavour. It only needs to be lightly cooked – overcooking will make it tough. Adding cranberry sauce and fresh thyme to the sauce gives a lovely fresh flavour to the classic combination of liver and sherry.

Serves 4

400 g (14 oz) sliced calf's liver

2 tbsp plain flour

400 g (14 oz) pappardelle or other wide flat noodles

1 tbsp sunflower oil

15 g (½ oz) butter

6 tbsp dry sherry

300 ml (10 fl oz) beef stock

2 tbsp cranberry sauce

2 tbsp tomato purée

½ tbsp chopped fresh thyme

75 g (2½ oz) watercress, roughly chopped

salt and pepper

Preparation and cooking time: about 20 minutes

1 Place the liver on a plate, pat dry with kitchen paper and snip off any gristly pieces with scissors. Mix the flour with some salt and pepper on another plate. Dip the liver in the seasoned flour until coated on both sides. Shake off the excess flour.

2 Cook the pasta in boiling water for 10–12 minutes, or according to the packet instructions, until al dente.

3 Meanwhile, heat the oil and butter in a non-stick frying pan and gently fry the liver over a moderate heat for 3–4 minutes, turning once. Transfer the liver to a plate and keep warm.

4 Add the sherry to the pan and allow to bubble for 1 minute or until reduced to half the quantity. Stir in the stock, cranberry sauce, tomato purée and thyme, and add salt and pepper to taste. Reduce the heat and cook for 4–5 minutes. Return the liver to the pan and heat through gently for 1–2 minutes.

5 Drain the pasta and mix with the watercress. Serve with the liver.

Some more ideas

● Use thinly sliced lamb's liver, and redcurrant jelly in place of the cranberry sauce. This is delicious with garlicky beans: drain and rinse a can of haricot beans, about 410 g, and warm through gently with 1 tbsp extra virgin olive oil, 1 crushed garlic clove and lots of chopped parsley.

● Instead of pasta, serve the liver with mashed potatoes, stirring the chopped watercress into the potatoes after mashing.

Plus points

● Liver is an excellent source of iron, zinc, copper, vitamin A and several of the B vitamins. It also offers useful amounts of vitamin D.

● Being a starchy carbohydrate, pasta provides energy and is a very satisfying food. It scores healthily low on the Glycaemic Index, which means that it breaks down slowly into glucose and glycogen in the body, so helping to prevent between-meal hunger pangs.

Each serving provides

kcal 625, **protein** 34 g, **fat** 15 g (of which saturated fat 5 g), **carbohydrate** 88 g (of which sugars 6 g), **fibre** 4 g

✓✓✓	A, B$_2$, B$_6$, B$_{12}$, niacin, copper, iron, zinc
✓✓	C, folate, selenium
✓	B$_1$, calcium

Steamed sea bass fillets with spring vegetables

Oriental steamer baskets are most handy for this dish – you can stack them so that everything can be steamed together. The moist heat from steaming ensures that the fish doesn't dry out. If using a liquid fish stock base or a cube, make up the stock half strength as it will get a lot of flavour from the marinade.

Serves 4

1 tsp grated fresh root ginger

1 tbsp light soy sauce

½ tsp toasted sesame oil

1 garlic clove, finely chopped

1 tbsp dry sherry, dry white wine or vermouth

4 sea bass fillets, 3.5 cm (1¼ in) thick, about 140 g (5 oz) each

700 ml (24 fl oz) fish stock

200 g (7 oz) couscous

1 strip of lemon zest

225 g (8 oz) baby carrots

12 spring onions, trimmed to about 10 cm (4 in) long

200 g (7 oz) asparagus tips

2 tbsp chopped parsley

salt and pepper

Preparation and cooking time: 30 minutes

Each serving provides

kcal 320, **protein** 34 g, **fat** 5 g (of which saturated fat 1 g), **carbohydrate** 35 g (of which sugars 8 g), **fibre** 3 g

✓✓✓	A, B₁₂
✓✓	C, folate, calcium, iron
✓	B₁, B₆

1 First make the marinade. Combine the ginger, soy sauce, sesame oil, garlic and sherry, wine or vermouth in a bowl. Add the fish and turn to coat in the marinade. Set aside.

2 Bring 250 ml (8½ fl oz) of the stock to the boil in a saucepan that will accommodate the steamer basket(s). Put the couscous in a bowl and pour over the boiling stock. Cover and leave to stand for about 15 minutes or until the couscous has swelled and absorbed the liquid.

3 Pour the remaining stock into the saucepan. Add the lemon zest and bring to the boil. Add the carrots. Reduce the heat so the stock simmers.

4 Place the fish, skin side down, in a single layer in a steamer basket. Add the spring onions and asparagus, or put them in a second stacking steamer basket. Place the steamer basket(s) over the gently boiling stock and cover. Steam for 10–12 minutes or until the fish is opaque throughout and begins to flake, and the vegetables are tender.

5 When the couscous is ready, add the parsley and fluff the grains with a fork to mix the couscous and parsley. Season with salt and pepper to taste.

6 Lift the steamer basket(s) off the pan. Drain the carrots, reserving the cooking liquid. Arrange the fish, carrots and steamed vegetables on warm plates with the couscous. Discard the lemon zest from the cooking liquid. Moisten the fish, vegetables and couscous with a little of the liquid, and serve with any remaining liquid as a sauce.

Plus points

● White fish such as sea bass are low in fat and calories and they offer many B-complex vitamins. Sea bass is also a good source of calcium, an essential mineral with many important functions in the body, including keeping bones and teeth strong.

● The active ingredient in asparagus, called asparagine, has a strong diuretic effect. Herbalists recommend eating asparagus as a treatment for rheumatism, arthritis and the bloating associated with PMT.

Some more ideas

- If you don't have a steamer, place the fish and vegetables in a colander, place inside a large pan and cover with a lid.
- Use salmon or cod fillets instead of sea bass. The cooking time may need to be reduced by a minute or 2 for thinner fish fillets; check for doneness after 8–9 minutes.

- For a simpler dish, omit the marinade and use water instead of fish stock. When the water comes to the boil, add 600 g (1 lb 5 oz) small new potatoes. Scatter 2 finely slivered small leeks and the finely grated zest of 1 lemon over the fish, then steam it over the potatoes. Meanwhile, cook 500 g (1 lb 2 oz) spinach until wilted; squeeze out excess water and chop.

Moisten with 4 tbsp single cream and season with salt and pepper to taste. Serve the fish on the creamed spinach, with the potatoes tossed with chopped fresh herbs.

- Instead of couscous, serve the fish with mashed potatoes. Use some of the fish cooking liquid instead of milk for mashing the potatoes and finish with a small knob of butter.

Stir-fried squid with spaghetti

There's no need to go out to eat when special dishes such as this are so easy to prepare at home. Black spaghetti coloured with squid ink, available from delicatessens and larger supermarkets, makes a great talking point.

Serves 4

450 g (1 lb) cleaned squid, rinsed and drained

1 tbsp extra virgin olive oil

1 onion, finely chopped

1 large fresh red chilli, seeded and finely chopped

280 g (10 oz) courgettes, cubed

2 garlic cloves, crushed

500 g (1 lb 2 oz) ripe plum tomatoes, diced

100 ml (3½ fl oz) red wine

4 tsp tomato purée

2 tsp sugar

400 g (14 oz) spaghetti, preferably black squid-ink spaghetti

small bunch of fresh basil, about 15 g (½ oz)

salt and pepper

Preparation and cooking time: 30 minutes

Each serving provides

kcal 530, **protein** 32 g, **fat** 7 g (of which saturated fat 1 g), **carbohydrate** 87 g (of which sugars 14 g), **fibre** 5 g

✓✓✓	B_6, B_{12}, selenium
✓✓	B_1, C, E, folate, copper, iron, potassium, zinc
✓	niacin, calcium

1 Separate the tentacles from the squid bodies. Trim the base of each tentacle and set aside on a plate. Cut the bodies into thin rings.

2 Heat the oil in deep frying pan, add the onion and chilli, and fry over a high heat for 3 minutes, stirring, until lightly browned. Add the squid rings, the courgettes and garlic. Stir-fry for 3 minutes or until the squid rings are opaque.

3 Add the tomatoes, wine, tomato purée and sugar, and season with salt and pepper to taste. Stir well, then leave to simmer for 5 minutes.

4 Meanwhile, cook the spaghetti in a large saucepan of boiling water for 10–12 minutes, or according to the packet instructions, until al dente.

5 Add the squid tentacles to the sauce. Reserve a few sprigs of basil for garnish, and tear the remaining leaves into the sauce. Cook for about 2 minutes or until the tentacles are just cooked and opaque.

6 Drain the spaghetti and divide among 4 plates. Spoon the squid and sauce over and garnish with the reserved basil leaves.

Some more ideas

- Toss the drained spaghetti with the squid and sauce before serving.
- The squid is also delicious served over rice.
- For seafood in piquant tomato sauce with penne, use 280 g (10 oz) skinless cod fillet, cut into 8 pieces, and 6 queen scallops, about 85 g (3 oz) in total, halved crossways through the coral. Make the tomato sauce as in the main recipe, but omitting the chilli and using fish stock instead of wine. In step 3, after seasoning, add the cod together with 2 tsp capers. Cover and simmer for 5 minutes. Add the scallops, cover again and simmer for a further 2–3 minutes. Serve on a bed of penne or other pasta shapes.

Plus points

- Squid is a good source of low-fat protein. It also offers excellent amounts of vitamin B_{12} and is rich in vitamin B_6 and selenium.
- Courgettes provide several B vitamins, including folate, niacin and B_6, as well as vitamin C and beta-carotene. It is important to eat the skins as they are the main source of these nutrients.

Asparagus risotto with truffle oil

Not only is risotto satisfying and delicious, it is a great vehicle for whatever fresh vegetables are in season. It needs plenty of stirring, but still takes only minutes to become perfectly cooked and creamy. A little truffle oil is a luxurious finishing touch for this risotto with fresh asparagus.

Serves 4

2 tbsp extra virgin olive oil

1 red onion, chopped

3 garlic cloves, chopped

350 g (12½ oz) risotto rice

250 ml (8½ fl oz) dry white wine

about 700 ml (24 fl oz) boiling vegetable stock

300 g (10½ oz) asparagus, cut into small pieces

1 tsp truffle oil

4 tbsp freshly grated Parmesan cheese

15 g (½ oz) softened butter, divided into 4 portions

2–3 tbsp snipped fresh chives

salt and pepper

Preparation and cooking time: 30 minutes

1 Heat the oil in a heavy-based pan and lightly sauté the onion and garlic for 2–3 minutes or until softened. Add the rice and cook over a moderately high heat for 1–2 minutes, stirring, until the rice is lightly toasted and golden brown in places.

2 Pour in the wine and stir until the rice has absorbed it. Add a small amount of stock and stir until it is absorbed. Continue gradually adding the stock, letting each amount be absorbed before adding the next, stirring frequently.

3 When the rice is almost al dente (after about 15 minutes), stir in the asparagus. Cook for a further 5 minutes or until the asparagus is tender and the rice is completely cooked. Continue adding stock during this time. The finished risotto should have a slightly soupy, almost creamy texture.

4 Remove from the heat. Season with salt and pepper to taste, and stir in the truffle oil and grated Parmesan. Spoon into warmed bowls, top each serving with a portion of butter and a sprinkling of chives, and serve.

Some more ideas

• When baby leeks are in season, make the risotto with 3–4 baby leeks, coarsely chopped, and 5 shallots, chopped, instead of asparagus.

• For a porcini and pea risotto with Parma ham, break up 10 g (¼ oz) dried porcini, rinse well to remove grit and add with the wine. In step 3, stir in 250 g (8½ oz) frozen petit pois in place of the asparagus. Omit the truffle oil and, instead of butter, garnish with 50 g (1¾ oz) Parma ham, cut into thin shreds.

• For a non-vegetarian dish, you can use chicken stock instead of vegetable stock.

Plus points

• Asparagus has been cultivated for over 2000 years and has been used medicinally since the 16th century. It is a rich source of many of the B vitamins, especially folate. A good intake of folate is important during the early stages of pregnancy to prevent birth defects such as spina bifida.

• Rice is one of the most important staple crops, the very basis of life for millions of people worldwide. It is an ideal food to include in a healthy diet as it is a low-fat starchy carbohydrate.

Each serving provides

kcal 575, **protein** 17 g, **fat** 18 g (of which saturated fat 6 g), **carbohydrate** 80 g (of which sugars 4 g), **fibre** 3 g

✓✓	A, B$_1$, B$_6$, C, folate, calcium, copper, iron, zinc
✓	E, niacin, potassium, selenium

Seared pork with kumquats

Here, thinly sliced pork fillet is quickly browned in a sizzling hot, ridged cast-iron grill pan, then simmered   with tangy kumquats, honey, Dijon mustard, white wine and stock. It is served on a bed of puréed potato, accompanied by crisp green beans, to make a very elegant dish.

Serves 4

675 g (1½ lb) floury potatoes, peeled and cut into chunks

340 g (12 oz) green beans

1 tbsp extra virgin olive oil

400 g (14 oz) pork fillet (tenderloin), thinly sliced

1 small onion, thinly sliced

115 g (4 oz) kumquats

1 tbsp clear honey

1 tbsp Dijon mustard

150 ml (5 fl oz) dry white wine

150 ml (5 fl oz) vegetable stock

3 tbsp semi-skimmed milk

freshly grated nutmeg

salt and pepper

snipped fresh chives to garnish (optional)

Preparation and cooking time: 30 minutes

Each serving provides

kcal 380, protein 26 g, fat 11 g (of which saturated fat 3 g), carbohydrate 38 g (of which sugars 12 g), fibre 5 g

✓✓✓	B_1, B_6, B_{12}, C
✓✓	niacin, copper, iron, potassium, zinc
✓	B_2, folate, calcium, selenium

1 Cook the potatoes in a saucepan of boiling water for 15 minutes or until tender. Steam the green beans in a steamer basket or colander over the potato pan for the last 5 minutes of the cooking time.

2 Meanwhile, heat the oil in a large ridged cast-iron grill pan. Add the slices of pork in batches and fry over a very high heat for 1 minute on each side or until browned. Lift the slices out of the pan and set aside.

3 Add the onion to the pan and fry over a high heat for 3 minutes, stirring. Reduce the heat slightly, then return the pork to the pan and fry for a further 5 minutes.

4 Thinly slice the kumquats, skin and all. Add to the pan together with the honey and cook for 1 minute. Mix the mustard, wine and stock together, and pour the mixture into the pan. Season with salt and pepper to taste and simmer for 3 minutes.

5 Drain the potatoes and mash them with the milk. Season with salt, pepper and nutmeg. Spoon the mashed potato into the centre of 4 serving plates. Arrange the pork slices on top of the mash and pour over a little of the sauce. Add the kumquats and beans and pour over the remaining sauce. Garnish with chives, if using.

Some more ideas

• Make a potato and celeriac mash by cooking 400 g (14 oz) celeriac, cut into 2 cm (¾ in) chunks, with 450 g (1 lb) potatoes.

• Use 4 duck breasts, about 1 kg (2¼ lb) in total, instead of the pork. Remove the skin and fat from the breasts. Halve each breast crossways, then cut through the thickness of each piece to make 4 thin slices. Fry as for the pork. In step 4, add a 2.5 cm (1 in) piece fresh root ginger, finely chopped, in place of the mustard. Serve with mash – either potato and celeriac or potato and carrot or swede – and green beans or steamed pak choy.

Plus points

• Pork, in common with all meat, is an excellent source of zinc. It also provides useful amounts of iron and the B vitamins, particularly B_1, B_6, B_{12} and niacin. Most cuts are now so lean that they have the same amount of fat as cottage cheese.

• Like all citrus fruit, kumquats are an excellent source of vitamin C. Because they are eaten with their skin they are also a useful source of fibre – weight for weight kumquats provide twice as much fibre as oranges.

Aromatic beef curry

This will satisfy even the most demanding curry addict. Lean and tender sirloin steak is quickly cooked with lots of spices, tomatoes, mushrooms and spinach, with yogurt added to give a luxurious feel. Served with cardamom-spiced rice, it makes a really healthy and nutritious meal.

Serves 4

1 tbsp sunflower oil

1 large onion, thinly sliced

150 g (5½ oz) button mushrooms, sliced

400 g (14 oz) sirloin steak, trimmed of fat and cut into thin strips

1½ tsp bottled chopped root ginger in oil, drained

2 garlic cloves, crushed

½ tsp crushed dried chillies

2 tsp ground coriander

¼ tsp ground cardamom

½ tsp turmeric

¼ tsp grated nutmeg

1 can chopped tomatoes, about 400 g

1 tsp cornflour mixed with 1 tbsp water

300 g (10½ oz) plain whole-milk yogurt

1 tbsp clear honey

125 g (4½ oz) young spinach leaves

juice of ½ lime

2 tbsp chopped fresh coriander, plus extra leaves to garnish

Cardamom rice

340 g (12 oz) basmati rice, well rinsed

1 cinnamon stick

8 whole green cardamom pods, cracked

juice of ½ lemon

salt

Preparation time: 10 minutes
Cooking time: 20 minutes

1 Heat the oil in a large saucepan and add the onion and mushrooms. Cook over a high heat for 2 minutes or until the onion slices begin to colour.

2 Add the beef together with the ginger, garlic, chillies, ground coriander, cardamom, turmeric and nutmeg. Cook for 2 minutes, stirring well, then add the tomatoes with their juice and the cornflour mixture. Bring to the boil, stirring. Stir in the yogurt and honey. Bring back to the boil, then reduce the heat, cover and simmer gently for 20 minutes.

3 Meanwhile, prepare the cardamom rice. Put 450 ml (15 fl oz) cold water in a saucepan and bring to the boil. Add the rice, cinnamon stick and cardamom pods. Bring back to the boil, then cover tightly and cook for 10 minutes or until the rice is tender. Drain off any excess water and return the rice to the saucepan. Stir in the lemon juice and keep covered until the curry is ready to serve.

4 Stir the spinach, lime juice and chopped coriander into the curry and allow the leaves to wilt down into the sauce. To serve, spoon the curry over the rice and garnish with fresh coriander leaves.

Plus points

- Cardamom is believed to be helpful for digestive problems, such as indigestion, flatulence and stomach cramps.
- Mushrooms are low in fat and calories and provide useful amounts of the B vitamins niacin, B_6 and folate. They are also a good source of copper.
- Along with its many other nutritional benefits, beef provides vitamins from the B group and is a useful source of vitamin D, which is found in relatively few foods.

Each serving provides

kcal 590, **protein** 36 g, **fat** 11 g (of which saturated fat 4 g), **carbohydrate** 86 g (of which sugars 16 g), **fibre** 2 g

✓✓✓	iron, zinc
✓✓	A, B_6, B_{12}, C, calcium, copper, potassium
✓	B_1, B_2, E, folate, selenium

Some more ideas

• If you like a hot curry, add a halved fresh red chilli to the sauce towards the end of the cooking time. The chilli can be left in the sauce or discarded before serving.

• Make a Thai-style pork and potato curry. Soften the onion and garlic in the oil with 200 g (7 oz) new potatoes, scrubbed and cut into small cubes, for 5 minutes. Stir in 300 g (10½ oz) pork fillet (tenderloin), thinly sliced, and 2 tbsp Thai red curry paste. Cook for 2 minutes or until browned. Add the canned chopped tomatoes, 150 ml (5 fl oz) vegetable stock and 100 g (3½ oz) ready-to-eat dried apricots, chopped. Bring to the boil, then cover and simmer for 20 minutes or until the pork is tender. Mix ½ tsp cornflour with 1 tbsp cold water and stir into the curry with 150 g (5½ oz) plain whole-milk yogurt, 1 tsp caster sugar and the spinach. Cook until the leaves wilt down into the sauce, then serve on plain rice.

Pappardelle with aubergine

A good but quick tomato sauce can turn a plate of pasta and aubergine into a delicious supper dish. The inspiration comes from Catania, in the shadow of Mount Etna in Sicily, where aubergine and tomato pasta is known as pasta alla Norma, in honour of the town's famous son, Bellini, and his opera, Norma.

Serves 4

6 tsp extra virgin olive oil

1 aubergine, unpeeled, cut crossways into 3–5 mm (⅛–¼ in) slices

3–4 garlic cloves, thinly sliced

2 cans chopped tomatoes, about 400 g each

400 g (14 oz) pappardelle or other wide flat noodles

2 tbsp tomato purée

¼ tsp sugar, or to taste

¼ tsp dried oregano, or to taste

salt and cayenne pepper

100 g (3½ oz) goat's cheese, sliced

15 g (½ oz) chopped parsley or torn fresh basil leaves to garnish

Preparation and cooking time: 25 minutes

Each serving provides

kcal 500, **protein** 18 g, **fat** 12 g (of which saturated fat 4 g), **carbohydrate** 85 g (of which sugars 10 g), **fibre** 6 g

✓✓	C, E, copper, iron
✓	A, B₁, B₆, B₁₂, folate, niacin, calcium, potassium, selenium, zinc

1 Heat a ridged cast-iron grill pan, then brush with 2 tsp of the olive oil. Arrange the aubergine slices in the pan and cook for 3–4 minutes. Brush the top side of the slices with another 2 tsp oil and turn them over. Cook for another 3–4 minutes or until tender and browned. Remove from the heat and cover lightly with a piece of foil to keep warm.

2 While the aubergine is cooking, heat the remaining 2 tsp olive oil in a heavy-based frying pan. Add the garlic and cook for 1–2 minutes or until just turning golden (do not let it brown or burn). Add the tomatoes with their juice. Cook over a high heat for 4–5 minutes, then reduce the heat to moderate and cook for a further 4–5 minutes, stirring ocasionally, until reduced to a thick sauce.

3 Meanwhile, cook the pappardelle in boiling water for 10–12 minutes, or according to the packet instructions, until al dente.

4 Add the tomato purée, sugar and oregano to the tomato sauce. Season with salt and cayenne pepper to taste. Keep warm.

5 Drain the pasta, turn it into the sauce and lightly toss to mix. Serve the pasta with the aubergine and goat's cheese, garnished with parsley or basil.

Another idea

● Try farfalle with grilled vegetables and green herb pesto. Arrange 1 courgette, cut into diagonal slices, 1 red or yellow pepper, seeded and sliced, 1 red onion, cut into wedges, 2 large ripe tomatoes, cut into wedges, and 12–16 tiny portabellini mushrooms or button mushrooms on a baking tray. Brush them with 1 tsp extra virgin olive oil, and grill under a moderate heat until tender and lightly browned in places. Meanwhile, make the pesto. In a food processor or blender, purée 170 g (6 oz) cooked spinach, squeezed dry, with 1 peeled garlic clove, 50 g (1¾ oz) mixed fresh herbs (primarily basil, with some chives, marjoram and flat-leaf parsley) and 2 tbsp extra virgin olive oil until smooth. Add the juice of ½ lemon and season with salt to taste. Cook 400 g (14 oz) farfalle (pasta bows); drain and toss with the pesto. Pile the grilled vegetables on top and sprinkle with 45 g (1½ oz) freshly grated Parmesan cheese.

Plus point

● Aubergine is a satisfyingly filling vegetable that is low in calories and fat. Grilling or baking is a healthy way to cook aubergine, which is renowned for absorbing large amounts of fat when fried.

Turkey escalopes with chestnut mushrooms and Madeira

Lean and tender turkey escalopes – breast steaks pounded until thin – only need brief cooking. Simmered with firm-textured chestnut mushrooms and a Madeira sauce finished with crème fraîche, they make a dish that is perfect for easy entertaining. Serve with basmati rice and a leafy salad.

Serves 4

4 small skinless turkey breast steaks, about 115 g (4 oz) each

2 tbsp plain flour

1 tbsp sunflower oil

25 g (scant 1 oz) butter

1 small onion, finely chopped

250 g (8½ oz) chestnut mushrooms, sliced

4 tbsp Madeira

2 tsp wholegrain mustard

1 tbsp chopped fresh oregano or 1 tsp dried oregano

150 ml (5 fl oz) chicken or turkey stock

2 tbsp crème fraîche

salt and pepper

2 tbsp chopped parsley to garnish

Preparation time: 15 minutes
Cooking time: 15 minutes

Each serving provides

kcal 355, **protein** 43 g, **fat** 13 g (of which saturated fat 6 g), **carbohydrate** 13 g (of which sugars 2 g), **fibre** 1.5 g

✓✓✓	copper
✓✓	B₆, B₁₂, C, niacin, Iron
✓	B₂, E, folate, potassium, zinc

1 Put the turkey steaks between sheets of cling film and pound them to flatten to about 5 mm (¼ in) thickness. Mix the flour with some salt and pepper, and use to coat the escalopes, shaking off the excess.

2 Heat the oil and butter in a large frying pan. Add the turkey escalopes, in one layer, and fry for 2–3 minutes on each side. Transfer the turkey to a plate and keep warm.

3 Add the onion to the pan and soften gently for 2–3 minutes. Add the mushrooms and cook for a further 1 minute or until softened.

4 Stir in the Madeira and allow to bubble for about 2 minutes, then stir in the mustard, oregano and stock. Return the escalopes to the pan and simmer gently for 3–4 minutes.

5 Using a draining spoon, spoon the turkey and mushrooms onto a warm serving platter. Stir the crème fraîche into the sauce and warm through, then check the seasoning. Pour the sauce over the turkey, sprinkle with parsley and serve.

Some more ideas

● Use veal escalopes or slices of pork fillet (tenderloin) in place of the turkey.

● Replace the mushrooms with 2 sliced courgettes, and use sherry instead of the Madeira.

● For a smart-occasion version, use a mixture of mushrooms, such as smoky-flavoured shiitake, subtle oyster mushrooms and whole baby button mushrooms.

Plus points

● Turkey has even less fat than chicken. Their nutritional profiles are similar, although turkey contains slightly more vitamin B₁₂, niacin and zinc.

● There are 2500 varieties of mushrooms grown around the world, though not all of them are edible. Mushrooms are low in fat and calories, with 0.5 g fat and 13 kcal in 100 g (3½ oz)

Sirloin steaks with port sauce

Thin sirloin steaks, sometimes sold as minute steaks, can be quickly fried, and the juices left in the pan turned into an instant sauce with the help of a little port. A colourful stir-fry of tiny new potatoes, mushrooms, red pepper and sugarsnap peas is a perfect accompaniment.

Serves 4

500 g (1 lb 2 oz) miniature new potatoes, scrubbed and any larger ones halved

1 tbsp extra virgin olive oil

250 g (8½ oz) large mushrooms, quartered

250 g (8½ oz) sugarsnap peas

1 large red pepper, seeded and cut into thin strips

180 ml (6 fl oz) beef or vegetable stock

1 tbsp Worcestershire sauce

1 tsp Dijon mustard

½ tsp dark brown muscovado sugar

4 thin sirloin steaks, about 140 g (5 oz) each, trimmed of fat

20 g (¾ oz) butter

1 shallot, finely chopped

2 garlic cloves, crushed

4 tbsp port

salt and pepper

Preparation and cooking time: 30 minutes

Each serving provides

kcal 420, **protein** 38 g, **fat** 15 g (of which saturated fat 6 g), **carbohydrate** 31 g (of which sugars 11 g), **fibre** 4.5 g

✓✓✓	A, B$_6$, B$_{12}$, C, zinc
✓✓	B$_1$, B$_2$, folate, niacin, copper, iron, potassium
✓	selenium

1 Put the potatoes in a saucepan and cover with boiling water. Bring back to the boil, then reduce the heat and simmer for 10–12 minutes.

2 Meanwhile, heat the oil in a wok or large frying pan (preferably non-stick), add the mushrooms, peas and pepper strips, and stir-fry for 1 minute. Mix 120 ml (4 fl oz) of the stock with the Worcestershire sauce, mustard and sugar, and stir into the vegetables. Reduce the heat and simmer gently for 3 minutes or until the vegetables are just tender, stirring frequently.

3 Season the steaks on both sides with coarsely ground black pepper and set aside. Heat a ridged cast-iron grill pan. Meanwhile, drain the cooked potatoes and add to the vegetables. Stir gently, then cover and leave over a very low heat until ready to serve.

4 Put the butter into the hot grill pan and turn up the heat to high. As soon as the butter sizzles and starts to foam, add the steaks. The cooking time depends on the thickness of the meat and whether you like your steaks rare, medium or well-done. For steaks 1 cm (½ in) thick, allow 1 minute on each side for rare (it will feel springy when pressed), 1½–2 minutes on each side for medium (it will feel slightly resistant when pressed), and 2½–3 minutes on

each side for well done (the meat will feel firm when pressed). Lift the steaks onto warmed dinner plates. Keep warm while making the sauce.

5 Add the shallot and garlic to the cooking juices in the pan and cook, stirring, over a low heat for 1 minute. Pour in the port and increase the heat so the sauce is bubbling. Cook for about 1 minute, stirring. Pour in the remaining stock and let it bubble for a minute. Check the seasoning. Spoon the sauce over the steaks and serve immediately, with the vegetables.

Plus point

● New potatoes are rich in vitamin C – which helps the absorption of iron from the beef – and the B vitamin folate. The preparation method makes a big difference to the amount of dietary fibre provided: new potatoes cooked in their skins offer one-third more fibre than peeled potatoes. Cooking potatoes in their skins also preserves the nutrients found just under the skin.

fast food for friends

Some more ideas

- Use a full-bodied red wine instead of the port.
- Fillet steaks, about 2.5 cm (1 in) thick, can be used instead of sirloin. Being thicker, fillet will need double the cooking time.

- For a less piquant vegetable stir-fry, omit the Worcestershire sauce, mustard and sugar, and toss the vegetables with 2 tbsp snipped fresh chives just before serving.
- For lamb steaks with rosemary wine sauce,

use 4 thinly cut boneless lean lamb leg steaks, about 140 g (5 oz) each. Allow an extra 1–2 minutes of cooking. For the sauce, use dry white wine instead of port and stir in 1 tsp chopped fresh rosemary.

Desserts in a Dash

Fruity desserts for every occasion

Fresh fruit makes the quickest and healthiest of desserts, and spices and other flavourings can transform all kinds of fruit into a tantalising treat in a trice. For a simple yet very special dish, you can mix several tropical fruits together and just spoon passion fruit seeds and citrus juice over them. Or sprinkle a little cinnamon and brown sugar over banana and creamy yogurt and then caramelise under the grill. Try citrus fruit and dates flavoured with star anise and Campari, or mango and lemon cream in brandy snap baskets, or figs and raspberries with rosewater crème fraîche. And who could resist a chocolate soufflé with fragrant strawberries?

Cinnamon banana caramels

Any fruit – fresh, canned or frozen – can be used to make this instant version of crème brûlée. The fruit is simply topped with Greek-style yogurt – a lower-fat alternative to double cream, very handy to have in the fridge for serving with desserts – then topped with demerara sugar and grilled to a rich caramel topping.

Serves 4

4 bananas

¼ tsp ground cinnamon

300 g (10½ oz) Greek-style yogurt

4 tbsp demerara sugar

Preparation time: 8 minutes

Cooking time: 1 minute

1 Preheat the grill. Peel and slice the bananas, cutting each one into about 16 slices. Divide the slices among four 250 ml (8½ fl oz) ramekin dishes and sprinkle with the ground cinnamon. Spoon the yogurt over the banana slices to cover them completely. Sprinkle 1 tbsp of sugar evenly over each dessert.

2 Place the dishes on a baking sheet and put them under the grill. Cook for about 1 minute or until the sugar melts into the yogurt – keep watch to make sure that it does not burn. Remove from the grill and leave to cool for a few minutes before serving.

Some more ideas

• For a very low-fat dessert, use 0%-fat Greek-style yogurt.

• Instead of yogurt, you can use low-fat soft cheese, thick fromage frais or crème fraîche.

• Try chopped peaches or nectarines, or a mixture of summer fruits, prepared the same way. Plums, rhubarb, blackcurrants and gooseberries can also be used, but these fruits are best lightly stewed in the minimum amount of water until tender, then cooled before the yogurt topping goes on.

• To make a crunchy raspberry dessert, use 200 g (7 oz) fresh raspberries. Toast 2 tbsp medium oatmeal in a frying pan over a moderately high heat for 2–3 minutes, watching to make sure it does not burn. Stir into the yogurt along with 2 tbsp clear honey. Spoon over the raspberries and sprinkle with 25 g (scant 1 oz) toasted flaked almonds.

Plus points

• Bananas are great energy providers and one of the best sources of potassium (in terms of fruit), a mineral we need to keep a stable balance of water in our bodies. Apart from pure carbohydrate, bananas also provide fibre plus useful amounts of vitamins B_6 and C, magnesium and copper.

• Yogurt is a useful source of calcium and phosphorus for strong bones and teeth, as well as vitamins B_2, needed for releasing energy from food, and B_{12}, essential for a healthy nervous system. Yogurt can help to regulate the balance of the bacteria in the large bowel, which may help to protect against cancer of the colon.

Each serving provides Ⓥ

kcal 240, **protein** 6 g, **fat** 7 g (of which saturated fat 4 g), **carbohydrate** 40 g (of which sugars 38 g), **fibre** 1 g

✓ B_6, B_{12}

Raspberry and vanilla risotto

This sweet and creamy fruit risotto is a delicious way of introducing more grain into your diet, and can balance a meal when it follows a main course that does not contain much starchy carbohydrate. The fresh raspberries colour the pudding a lovely pale pink, as well as adding sweetness.

Serves 6

1 litre (1¾ pints) semi-skimmed milk
1 vanilla pod, split open in half
140 g (5 oz) risotto rice
1 strip lemon zest
3 tbsp golden caster sugar or light soft
    brown sugar
6 tbsp flaked almonds
200 g (7 oz) fresh raspberries
6 tbsp single cream
vanilla pods to decorate (optional)

Preparation and cooking time: 30 minutes

1 Pour the milk into a heavy-based saucepan and add the vanilla pod. Sprinkle in the rice, stirring constantly. Bring to the boil over a moderate heat, stirring, then reduce the heat so the mixture is gently simmering.

2 Add the lemon zest and sugar. Cook, stirring frequently, for 15–18 minutes or until the rice is suspended in the sauce and is tender, and the liquid is thick and creamy.

3 Meanwhile, put the almonds in a small non-stick frying pan and toast over a low heat for 4–5 minutes or until they are lightly browned.

4 When the risotto has finished cooking, remove the vanilla pod and lemon zest. Stir in half of the raspberries. Remove from the heat and continue stirring for 1–2 minutes or until the fruit softens and begins to turn the risotto pink.

5 Spoon the raspberry risotto into 6 warmed bowls and drizzle 1 tbsp cream over each serving. Sprinkle the almonds over the top and add the remaining berries. Decorate with vanilla pods, if wished, and serve at once – the risotto thickens as it cools.

Another idea

● Make a sweet pudding with quinoa, an ancient grain used by the Incas. Available from healthfood shops, quinoa is rich in nutrients and has a high amino acid content. Rinse 125 g (4½ oz) quinoa and drain well, then toast in a frying pan, without any fat, for about 4 minutes, stirring frequently. It will become a deeper golden colour and pop regularly. Sprinkle the quinoa into the hot milk (heated without the vanilla pod), stirring. When the milk boils, reduce the heat so the mixture is bubbling very gently. Cover and cook for 10 minutes. Instead of flaked almonds, use 45 g (1½ oz) ground almonds and stir them into the quinoa. Continue cooking for about 20 minutes or until most of the milk has been absorbed, stirring occasionally. (The quinoa will retain a slight crunchy texture and have a lovely toasted flavour.) Stir in 1 tbsp clear honey with half of the raspberries, or serve them all on top of the pudding.

Plus point

● Almonds are a good source of vitamin E, which helps to protect against heart disease. They also contribute useful amounts of phosphorus, copper and magnesium.

Each serving provides

ⓥ

kcal 320, **protein** 11 g, **fat** 14 g (of which saturated fat 4 g), **carbohydrate** 38 g (of which sugars 19 g), **fibre** 2 g

✓✓ C, E, calcium

✓   B₂, B₁₂, copper, iron, zinc

Citrus salad with dates

Fresh dates are such a treat: sweet, succulent and tender. They are the perfect complement to grapefruit and orange in this refreshing vitamin C-rich dessert. With a syrup flavoured with star anise, Campari and some fresh mint, this offers a real taste sensation at the end of a meal.

Serves 4

2 tbsp clear honey

120 ml (4 fl oz) freshly squeezed citrus juice, such as orange and grapefruit

3 star anise

1 white grapefruit

1 pink grapefruit

2 oranges

1 blood orange or another pink grapefruit

2 tbsp Campari

6–8 fresh dates, stoned and halved

2 sprigs of fresh mint, stalks removed and leaves thinly sliced or chopped

Preparation time: 15–20 minutes

1 Combine the honey, citrus juice and star anise in a small saucepan. Bring to the boil over a moderate heat, then reduce the heat and simmer for 5–7 minutes or until slightly thickened.

2 Meanwhile, peel the citrus fruits, removing as much white pith as possible. Slice the fruits crossways, removing any pips. Arrange the citrus slices in a serving bowl.

3 Add the Campari to the syrup and cook for a further 1–2 minutes. Pour the hot syrup over the citrus slices. Arrange the halved dates over the top, then sprinkle with the mint. Leave the salad to macerate until ready to eat.

Some more ideas

● Instead of star anise, add a few drops of pure vanilla extract to the sauce at the end of cooking.

● This dessert is also good chilled, but serve within 3 hours of making, otherwise the fruit may start to break up.

● Turn this into a fruit and cheese course or a light lunch by adding some sliced feta or goat's cheese and serving with crusty bread.

● For a melon and fig salad with walnuts, peel and seed a medium-sized, ripe Charentais or Galia melon and cut into bite-sized slices. Add 6 diced dried figs and 45 g (1½ oz) walnut pieces. Make the syrup as in the main recipe, but using 3–5 sprigs of fresh thyme instead of star anise and omitting the Campari. Pour the syrup over the fruit and toss together, then add the juice of ½ lemon and a pinch of ground cinnamon. Toss once more and serve.

Plus points

● Pink grapefruit is a good source of lycopene, a phytochemical that can help to protect against cancer and heart disease.

● In dates, 95% of the energy content comes from natural sugars. As the sugars come wrapped in fibre, the body is able to control a slow and steady release of glucose into the blood stream.

Each serving provides ⓥ

kcal 150, **protein** 2 g, **fat** 0 g, **carbohydrate** 32 g (of which sugars 32 g), **fibre** 3 g

✓✓✓ C
✓✓ folate
✓ B$_1$, potassium

desserts in a dash

Sparkling peach dessert

For an almost instant, festive dessert at the height of summer, top ripe, juicy peaches with raspberry sorbet, ice-cold sparkling wine (Champagne is especially good, if you have some opened) and a sprinkling of chopped toasted nuts. If time allows, chill the wine glasses or dessert dishes first.

Serves 4

4 ripe peaches

4 scoops of raspberry sorbet, about 250 g (8½ oz) in total

8 tbsp sparkling white wine, well chilled

4 tbsp chopped toasted almonds

Preparation time: 10 minutes

1 Rinse the peaches and pat dry on kitchen paper. Halve each fruit and discard the stones. Using a small sharp knife, dice the flesh, then divide it among 4 wine glasses or dessert dishes.

2 Rinse an ice-cream scoop with hot water and use to scoop up the sorbet. Put a scoop on top of the peach in each glass.

3 Add 2 tbsp of sparkling wine to each glass, then sprinkle with the toasted almonds. Serve immediately.

Some more ideas

• If peaches are unavailable, ripe nectarines make a good substitute.

• When soft fruit is at its best, make a sparkling berry dessert. Use 300 g (10½ oz) strawberries, halved, or a mixture of raspberries and blueberries. You can use fruits of the forest sorbet instead of raspberry, or frozen vanilla yogurt or fruits of the forest yogurt.

• Replace the almonds with 4 tbsp chopped toasted hazelnuts.

• Instead of sparkling wine (or even Champagne), use a dessert wine such as Beaume de Venise.

• For a non-alcoholic alternative to sparkling wine, add 1 tbsp undiluted elderflower cordial to each serving.

Plus points

• Peaches are an excellent source of vitamin C (1 medium-sized peach provides around three-quarters of the recommended daily amount). They also provide useful amounts of fibre and are low in calories.

• Although sorbets can be quite high in calories because of the sugar they contain, they are much lower in fat than ice cream.

Each serving provides ⓥ

kcal 225, **protein** 5 g, **fat** 8 g (of which saturated fat 1 g), **carbohydrate** 30 g (of which sugars 30 g), **fibre** 3 g

✓✓✓	C
✓✓	E
✓	B₂, copper

Exotic fruit salad

This simple but very special fruit salad is just bursting with the wonderful colours and fragrance of exotic fruits – papaya, mango, kiwi fruit and passion fruit. It's rich in vitamins too, making a delightfully refreshing and nutritious end to a meal. Arrange the fruit on a platter or mix together in a pretty bowl.

Serves 4

1 large papaya
1 large mango
2 kiwi fruit
6 tbsp orange juice
2 tbsp lime juice
2 passion fruit

Preparation time: 15 minutes

1 Peel and halve the papaya and scoop out the seeds. Slice the fruit crossways and arrange the slices in 2 rows on a serving platter, or cut into chunks and put into a large serving bowl.

2 Stone and peel the mango and cut lengthways into wedges. Arrange the wedges in a row between the papaya slices. Or cut into chunks and add to the serving bowl.

3 Peel the kiwi fruit and cut lengthways into wedges or chunks. Scatter them over the slices of mango and papaya.

4 Mix the orange juice with the lime juice. Halve the passion fruit and scoop out the seeds and pulp into the juice mixture. Spoon over the salad and serve immediately.

Some more ideas

● Instead of using orange juice, make a syrup. Put 2 tbsp sugar in a small saucepan with 6 tbsp water and dissolve it over a low heat, then bring to the boil and boil for 2 minutes. Remove from the heat and add the lime juice. Allow the syrup to cool while preparing the fruit.

● For an orange, kiwi and strawberry salad, peel 2 oranges and cut into segments, holding them over a bowl to catch the juice. Mix the segments with 2 kiwi fruit, cut into wedges, and 280 g (10 oz) strawberries, halved or sliced if large. Warm the juice from segmenting the oranges (about 4 tbsp) with 2 tbsp maple syrup or honey until just combined, then cool. Add a handful of freshly torn basil leaves, and drizzle over the fruit.

● Sprinkle the salad with 2 tbsp toasted coconut shreds.

● Instead of the papaya and mango, use a small melon, such as Ogen, and about 400 g (14 oz) peeled pineapple.

Plus points

● Mango, papaya, kiwi and passion fruit are all excellent sources of vitamin C. An average slice of papaya provides more than double the recommended daily requirement of vitamin C, and the mango provides 6 times the daily requirement of vitamin C.

● All the fruits in this salad provide a wealth of phytochemicals that help to protect against excessive free radical attack, which may spark off degenerative diseases.

● As well as being an excellent source of vitamin C and beta-carotene, mango provides useful amounts of vitamin B_6.

Each serving provides Ⓥ

kcal 120, **protein** 2 g, **fat** 0.5 g (of which saturated fat 0 g), **carbohydrate** 27 g (of which sugars 19 g), **fibre** 5 g

✓✓✓ C

✓✓ A, B_6, potassium

desserts in a dash

Hot fruity parcels

\Baking fruit in paper parcels is a brilliant way of sealing in all the flavour and preserving the precious nutrients. It also makes a novel presentation method and saves on washing up! Serve this delicious fruity treat of fresh pineapple and dried apricots with a dollop of Greek-style yogurt or crème fraîche.

Serves 4

1 ripe pineapple

12 ready-to-eat dried apricots

2 tsp cardamom pods

grated zest of 1 orange

4 tbsp orange juice

4 tsp clear honey

55 g (2 oz) good plain chocolate (at least 70% cocoa solids), grated

Preparation time: 10 minutes

Cooking time: 20 minutes

1 Preheat the oven to 200°C (400°F, gas mark 6). Cut 4 sheets of baking parchment or greaseproof paper, each measuring about 30 cm (12 in) square.

2 Peel the pineapple and cut out the core. Cut the flesh into slices and then into cubes. Divide the cubes among the squares of paper and add 3 apricots to each one. Crush the cardamom pods and extract the seeds. Add to the parcels. Sprinkle over the orange zest and juice, and drizzle 1 tsp honey on top of each.

3 Wrap the paper loosely round the fruit, enclosing it completely, and seal tightly. Place the parcels on a baking tray and bake for 20 minutes.

4 Place the parcels on individual serving plates and unwrap them. Sprinkle grated chocolate into each parcel and serve.

Some more ideas

● Save time by using a tub of ready-sliced fresh pineapple in pineapple juice, about 350 g, drained.

● The fruit can be varied according to what is in season or what you have available. For example, instead of apricots use halved strawberries or thickly sliced firm bananas.

● For pear and cranberry parcels, use 4 peeled, cored and quartered ripe dessert pears and 85 g (3 oz) sweetened dried cranberries. Add a

piece of cinnamon stick to each parcel in place of the cardamom seeds. Bake for about 15 minutes. After cooking, unwrap the parcels and sprinkle a few chopped walnuts over instead of the chocolate.

● For a special occasion, spoon 1 tsp brandy, Cointreau or Grand Marnier into each parcel in place of the orange juice and serve with good-quality vanilla ice cream.

● The parcels, made using foil instead of parchment or greaseproof paper, can be cooked on a barbecue for 5 minutes.

Each serving provides

Ⓥ

kcal 230, **protein** 3 g, **fat** 4 g (of which saturated fat 2 g), **carbohydrate** 48 g (of which sugars 48 g), **fibre** 5 g

✓✓✓	C
✓✓	D_1, D_6, copper, potassium
✓	B_2, folate

Plus points

● Dried apricots are one of the richest fruit sources of iron. They also provide useful amounts of vitamin A (derived from beta-carotene) and fibre.

● Pineapple contains an enzyme called bromelin, which aids digestion. It is also a good source of vitamin C.

Nectarine and currant tarts

Summer fruit tarts always look so appealing, and here a combination of thinly sliced nectarines with red, white and black currants provides a vivid contrast of colours, textures and flavours. Using sheets of ready-made filo pastry for the tart cases makes the preparation simple.

Serves 4

4 sheets filo pastry, 48 x 29 cm (19 x 11½ in) each, about 135 g (4¾ oz) in total, thawed if frozen

30 g (1 oz) unsalted butter, melted

2 ripe nectarines

150 g (5½ oz) mixed fresh red, white and black currants

2 tbsp apricot conserve

1 tbsp apple or orange juice

icing sugar for dusting

Preparation time: 20 minutes
Cooking time: 8–10 minutes

Each serving provides Ⓥ

kcal 170, **protein** 4 g, **fat** 5 g (of which saturated fat 3 g), **carbohydrate** 27 g (of which sugars 14 g), **fibre** 2 g

| ✓✓✓ | C |
| ✓ | A |

1 Preheat the oven to 180°C (350°F, gas mark 4). Grease 4 cups in a muffin tray (each cup should measure 7.5 cm/3 in diameter and be 3 cm/1¼ in deep).

2 Working with one sheet of filo at a time and keeping the rest covered with a damp tea towel, cut each sheet into 6 squares measuring about 15 cm (6 in). Use 6 squares of filo (1 whole sheet) for each tart case.

3 Brush one square very lightly with some of the melted butter, then arrange another square on top, set at a slightly different angle. Brush lightly with butter, then stack on the remaining 4 squares, arranging each at a different angle and brushing lightly with butter. Press gently into one of the cups in the muffin tray. Repeat to make 3 more filo cases. Brush the cases with any remaining butter.

4 Halve the nectarines and remove the stones, then thinly slice. Arrange the slices in the filo cases, on one side, placing them almost vertical in a fan shape. Add the currants on the other side to fill the pastry cases.

5 Bake for 8–10 minutes or until the pastry is golden. Meanwhile, gently warm the apricot conserve with the apple or orange juice until melted and smooth.

6 Allow the tarts to cool in the muffin cups for 5 minutes, then carefully remove and arrange on a serving platter. Gently brush the warm apricot mixture over the fruit to glaze. Dust the tarts with icing sugar. Eat warm, or at room temperature within 2 hours of baking.

Some more ideas

• Instead of nectarines you can use ripe peaches or slices of fresh mango, and fresh blueberries in place of currants.

• A mixture of chopped ready-to-eat dried fruit, such as apricots, figs and apple slices, about 150 g (5½ oz), can be used instead of the nectarines, and raisins, sultanas or currants in place of fresh currants.

Plus points

• Fresh currants and nectarines both provide vitamin C – currants are an excellent source. Nectarines also offer B-complex vitamins and the antioxidant beta-carotene.

• Unlike most other types of pastry, filo contains very little fat – only 4 g in 100 g (3½ oz) compared to 29 g fat in the same weight of shortcrust pastry. Being sparing with the butter for brushing keeps the total fat content healthily low.

Chocolate and hazelnut soufflés

These luscious soufflés are surprisingly easy to prepare and make an impressive special occasion dessert, with far less fat than the traditional version. For best results, use a good-quality chocolate.

Serves 6

2 tsp unsalted butter

30 g (1 oz) amaretti biscuits, finely crushed

240 ml (8 fl oz) semi-skimmed milk

few drops of pure vanilla extract

3 tbsp cornflour

55 g (2 oz) ground hazelnuts

100 g (3½ oz) good plain chocolate (at least 70% cocoa solids), broken into small pieces

2 egg yolks

1 tbsp hazelnut or almond liqueur

4 egg whites

pinch of cream of tartar or salt

85 g (3 oz) caster sugar

500 g (1 lb 2 oz) strawberries, halved

1 tbsp icing sugar for dusting (optional)

Preparation time: 15 minutes
Cooking time: 15 minutes

Each serving provides　　ⓥ

kcal 340, **protein** 8 g, **fat** 16 g (of which saturated fat 5 g), **carbohydrate** 44 g (of which sugars 34 g), **fibre** 1.5 g

✓✓✓	C
✓✓	B₂, B₆, E
✓	calcium, copper, iron

1 Preheat the oven to 180°C (350°F, gas mark 4). Grease six 200 ml (7 fl oz) ramekins or ovenproof cups with the butter and coat with amaretti biscuit crumbs, turning the dishes to cover the insides evenly.

2 Put the milk and vanilla extract into a saucepan and bring just to the boil. Remove from the heat. Put the cornflour and ground hazelnuts in a mixing bowl and whisk in a little of the hot milk, a spoonful at a time, to make a thick paste. Slowly whisk in enough of the remaining milk to make a smooth, thick liquid, then whisk in the remainder. Pour the mixture back into the saucepan and bring to the boil, stirring. Boil gently for 2–4 minutes or until thickened.

3 Remove from the heat and add the chocolate. Cover the pan and leave to stand for 1–2 minutes or until the chocolate has melted. Stir to combine well. Whisk in the egg yolks, one at a time, and then the hazelnut or almond liqueur.

4 Put the egg whites in a large, clean, greasefree bowl with the cream of tartar or salt. Using an electric mixer or balloon whisk, whisk the egg whites until they form soft peaks, then add the sugar a spoonful at a time, whisking well. Continue whisking until glossy and forming stiff peaks.

5 Stir a spoonful of the egg whites into the chocolate mixture to lighten it, then pour this mixture over the rest of the whites. Using a large rubber spatula or metal spoon, gently fold together until just combined. (Don't worry about a few white streaks.)

6 Scrape the soufflé mixture into the prepared dishes or cups and bake for 15 minutes or until puffed and lightly browned on top. Set the ramekins or cups on individual plates with the strawberries and, if you wish, dust each soufflé lightly with icing sugar. Serve immediately.

Plus points

• None of us needs to feel guilty about the occasional indulgence – as long as the rest of the diet is healthy. According to the organisation ARISE (Research into the Science of Enjoyment), there is scientific evidence that eating chocolate can be good for you. Studies suggest that people who Indulge once In a whlle tend to be more relaxed and happier, and medical evidence shows that happy people live longer.

Some more ideas

- Instead of amaretti biscuits, you can use finely crushed digestive biscuits.
- Use ground almonds instead of hazelnuts and almond liqueur instead of hazelnut; coffee liqueur could be substituted for either.
- For a lower-fat version, omit the egg yolks and increase the liqueur to 2 tbsp.
- Make a berry soufflé omelette to serve 4. Sprinkle 400 g (14 oz) sliced strawberries or

whole raspberries with 1–2 tbsp caster sugar and leave to macerate while you make the omelette. Preheat the grill to moderate. Separate 3 large eggs and beat the yolks with 2 tbsp caster sugar until thick and light in colour. Stir in 2 tbsp milk or orange liqueur and ¼ tsp pure vanilla extract. Whisk the egg whites until they form stiff peaks. Fold the egg yolk mixture gently into the whites. Melt 2 tsp butter in a non-stick frying pan, about 25 cm (10 in) in

diameter, with a heatproof handle (alternatively, wrap the handle with foil). Scrape the egg mixture into the frying pan and smooth the top. Cook over a low heat, without stirring, for 4–5 minutes or until the omelette is browned on the base. Put under the grill for 1½–2 minutes or until lightly browned on top and puffed up. Slide onto a warm plate and cut into quarters. Serve with the fruit spooned over.

- Substitute brandy for the liqueur.

Fragrant mango cream in brandy-snap baskets

What could be quicker than luscious fresh fruit blended with Greek-style yogurt and lemon curd, and spooned into ready-made brandy-snap baskets? This is a really special, creamy treat.

Serves 6

1 large ripe mango
2 passion fruit
2 tbsp good-quality lemon curd
300 g (10½ oz) Greek-style yogurt
6 brandy-snap baskets
1 tbsp chopped pistachio nuts
fresh mint leaves to decorate

Preparation time: 15 minutes

1 Cut the peel from the mango and slice the flesh from the flat stone. Place half the mango flesh in a food processor or blender and process briefly until smooth. Spoon into a bowl. Chop the remaining mango flesh into pieces and set aside.

2 Cut the passion fruit in half and scoop out the seeds and pulp into the mango purée. Stir in the lemon curd. Add the yogurt and fold everything together until well combined.

3 Spoon the fruit and yogurt cream into the brandy-snap baskets and top with the chopped mango. Scatter a few chopped pistachio nuts over the top of each serving and decorate with fresh mint leaves. Serve immediately.

Some more ideas

● Orange curd, which is becoming more widely available, makes a delicious alternative to lemon curd.
● Substitute a papaya for the mango.
● For a raspberry and chocolate cream on panettone, add 2 tbsp chopped toasted hazelnuts and 4 tbsp chocolate ice cream sauce to 300 g (10½ oz) Greek-style yogurt, and swirl together until the chocolate sauce has marbled the yogurt. Cut 3 long slices of dried fruit panettone in half and toast under the grill until golden. Spoon the chocolate cream over the panettone and scatter on 125 g (4½ oz) fresh raspberries. Dust lightly with icing sugar and serve decorated with fresh mint leaves.
● Slice 2 bananas and divide them among the brandy-snap baskets. Top with the chocolate and hazelnut cream above and finish with a fine drizzle of warm chocolate sauce.

Plus points

● Greek-style yogurt tastes luxurious, but has a fraction of the fat and calories of double cream: double cream contains 449 kcal and 48 g fat per 100 g (3½ oz), while the same weight of Greek-style yogurt has just 115 kcal and 9 g fat.
● The ancient Indians believed that mangoes helped to increase sexual desire and prolong love-making. Whether or not this is true, mangoes are rich in carotenoid compounds and vitamin C, both antioxidants that can help to protect against damage by free radicals. Mangoes also provide useful amounts of fibre and copper.

Each serving provides

kcal 220, protein 5 g, fat 11 g (of which saturated fat 3 g), carbohydrate 26 g (of which sugars 22 g), fibre 2 g

✓✓✓	C
✓✓	A
✓	B₂, B₁₂, calcium

desserts in a dash

153

Fresh figs with raspberries and rose cream

As well as being a superb end to a meal, this simple fruit dessert is also packed with fibre from both the figs and raspberries. Rosewater – which is available in supermarkets and delicatessens – is a popular flavouring in the Middle East and in parts of the Mediterranean. It is made from distilled rose petals and has an intense aroma.

Serves 4

8 small, ripe juicy figs

4 large fresh fig leaves (optional)

200 g (7 oz) fresh raspberries

fresh mint leaves to decorate

Rose cream

100 g (3½ oz) crème fraîche

2 tsp raspberry jam

finely grated zest of 1 lime

1–2 tbsp rosewater, or to taste

Preparation time: about 15 minutes

1 To make the rose cream, place the crème fraîche in a bowl and beat in the raspberry jam and lime zest until the jam is well distributed. Add the rosewater and stir to mix in. Transfer to a pretty serving bowl.

2 Cut each of the figs vertically into quarters without cutting all the way through, so they each remain whole. Arrange the fig leaves, if using, on 4 plates and place 2 figs on each plate.

3 Spoon a dollop of the rose cream into the centre of each fig; serve the remaining cream separately. Scatter the raspberries over the plates, decorate with the mint leaves and serve.

Some more ideas

• Stir 350 g (12 oz) sliced ripe strawberries into the rose cream.

• On the same theme, serve fresh peaches with an orange cream. To make the cream, flavour 100 g (3½ oz) crème fraîche with 2 tsp orange-blossom honey, the finely grated zest of ½ orange and 1–2 tbsp orange-flower water, to taste. For a special occasion, sprinkle in 1–2 tsp almond liqueur. Cut 4 large peaches in half and remove the stones. Place 2 halves on each plate and fill with the orange cream. Arrange fresh orange slices on the plates and grate a little nutmeg over both the peaches and the orange slices.

• For a quick dessert that is rich in vitamin C, fold 500 g (1 lb 2 oz) raspberries, blackberries, blueberries or halved strawberries into the rose or orange cream and spoon into dessert glasses (omit the figs).

• For a lower-fat dessert use reduced-fat crème fraîche.

Plus points

• Like all berries, raspberries are an excellent source of vitamin C – 100 g (3½ oz) provides around 80% of the recommended daily requirement. Raspberries also offer useful amounts of folate and dietary fibre.

• In addition to fibre, fresh figs offer small but not negligible amounts of many vitamins and minerals.

Each serving provides

kcal 150, **protein** 2 g, **fat** 10 g (of which saturated fat 6 g), **carbohydrate** 12 g (of which sugars 12 g), **fibre** 3 g

✓✓✓	C
✓	B₆

A glossary of nutritional terms

Antioxidants These are compounds that help to protect the body's cells against the damaging effects of free radicals. Vitamins C and E, beta-carotene (the plant form of vitamin A) and the mineral selenium, together with many of the phytochemicals found in fruit and vegetables, all act as antioxidants.

Calorie A unit used to measure the energy value of food and the intake and use of energy by the body. The scientific definition of 1 calorie is the amount of heat required to raise the temperature of 1 gram of water by 1 degree Centigrade. This is such a small amount that in this country we tend to use the term kilocalories (abbreviated to *kcal*), which is equivalent to 1000 calories. Energy values can also be measured in kilojoules (kJ): 1 kcal = 4.2 kJ.

A person's energy (calorie) requirement varies depending on his or her age, sex and level of activity. The estimated average daily energy requirements are:

Age (years)	Female (kcal)	Male (kcal)
1–3	1165	1230
4–6	1545	1715
7–10	1740	1970
11–14	1845	2220
15–18	2110	2755
19–49	1940	2550
50–59	1900	2550
60–64	1900	2380
65–74	1900	2330

Carbohydrates These energy-providing substances are present in varying amounts in different foods and are found in three main forms: sugars, starches and non-starch polysaccharides (NSP), usually called fibre.

There are two types of sugars: *intrinsic sugars*, which occur naturally in fruit (fructose) and sweet-tasting vegetables, and *extrinsic sugars*, which include lactose (from milk) and all the non-milk extrinsic sugars (NMEs) – sucrose (table sugar), honey, treacle, molasses and so on. The NMEs, or 'added' sugars, provide only calories, whereas foods containing intrinsic sugars also offer vitamins, minerals and fibre. Added sugars (*simple carbohydrates*) are digested and absorbed rapidly to provide energy very quickly. Starches and fibre (*complex carbohydrates*), on the other hand, break down more slowly to offer a longer-term energy source (see also Glycaemic Index). Starchy carbohydrates are found in bread, pasta, rice,

wholegrain and breakfast cereals, and potatoes and other starchy vegetables such as parsnips, sweet potatoes and yams.

Healthy eating guidelines recommend that at least half of our daily energy (calories) should come from carbohydrates, and that most of this should be from complex carbohydrates. No more than 11% of our total calorie intake should come from 'added' sugars. For an average woman aged 19–49 years, this would mean a total carbohydrate intake of 259 g per day, of which 202 g should be from starch and intrinsic sugars and no more than 57 g from added sugars. For a man of the same age, total carbohydrates each day should be about 340 g (265 g from starch and intrinsic sugars and 75 g from added sugars).

See also Fibre and Glycogen.

Cholesterol There are two types of cholesterol – the soft waxy substance called blood cholesterol, which is an integral part of human cell membranes, and dietary cholesterol, which is contained in food. *Blood cholesterol* is important in the formation of some hormones and it aids digestion. High blood cholesterol levels are known to be an important risk factor for coronary heart disease, but most of the cholesterol in our blood is made by the liver – only about 25% comes from cholesterol in food. So while it would seem that the amount of cholesterol-rich foods in the diet would have a direct effect on blood cholesterol levels, in fact the best way to reduce blood cholesterol is to eat less saturated fat and to increase intake of foods containing soluble fibre.

Fat Although a small amount of fat is essential for good health, most people consume far too much. Healthy eating guidelines recommend that no more than 33% of our daily energy intake (calories) should come from fat. Each gram of fat contains 9 kcal, more than twice as many calories as carbohydrate or protein, so for a woman aged 19–49 years this means a daily maximum of 71 g fat, and for a man in the same age range 93.5 g fat.

Fats can be divided into 3 main groups: saturated, monounsaturated and polyunsaturated, depending on the chemical structure of the fatty acids they contain. *Saturated fatty acids* are found mainly in animal fats such as butter and other dairy products and in fatty meat. A high intake of saturated fat is known to be a risk factor for coronary heart disease and certain types of cancer. Current guidelines are that no more than 10% of our daily calories should come from saturated fats, which is about 21.5 g for an adult woman and 28.5 g for a man.

Where saturated fats tend to be solid at room temperature, the *unsaturated fatty acids* –

monounsaturated and polyunsaturated – tend to be liquid. *Monounsaturated fats* are found predominantly in olive oil, groundnut (peanut) oil, rapeseed oil and avocados. Foods high in *polyunsaturates* include most vegetable oils – the exceptions are palm oil and coconut oil, both of which are saturated.

Both saturated and monounsaturated fatty acids can be made by the body, but certain polyunsaturated fatty acids – known as *essential fatty acids* – must be supplied by food. There are 2 'families' of these essential fatty acids: *omega-6*, derived from linoleic acid, and *omega-3*, from linolenic acid. The main food sources of the omega-6 family are vegetable oils such as olive and sunflower; omega-3 fatty acids are provided by oily fish, nuts, and vegetable oils such as soya and rapeseed.

When vegetable oils are hydrogenated (hardened) to make margarine and reduced-fat spreads, their unsaturated fatty acids can be changed into trans fatty acids, or '*trans fats*'. These artificially produced trans fats are believed to act in the same way as saturated fats within the body – with the same risks to health. Current healthy eating guidelines suggest that no more than 2% of our daily calories should come from trans fats, which is about 4.3 g for an adult woman and 5.6 g for a man. In thinking about the amount of trans fats you consume, remember that major sources are processed foods such as biscuits, pies, cakes and crisps.

Fibre Technically non-starch polysaccharides (NSP), fibre is the term commonly used to describe several different compounds, such as pectin, hemicellulose, lignin and gums, which are found in the cell walls of all plants. The body cannot digest fibre, nor does it have much nutritional value, but it plays an important role in helping us to stay healthy.

Fibre can be divided into 2 groups – soluble and insoluble. Both types are provided by most plant foods, but some foods are particularly good sources of one type or the other. *Soluble fibre* (in oats, pulses, fruit and vegetables) can help to reduce high blood cholesterol levels and to control blood sugar levels by slowing down the absorption of sugar. *Insoluble fibre* (in wholegrain cereals, pulses, fruit and vegetables) increases stool bulk and speeds the passage of waste material through the body. In this way it helps to prevent constipation, haemorrhoids and diverticular disease, and may protect against bowel cancer.

Our current intake of fibre is around 12 g a day. Healthy eating guidelines suggest that we need to increase this amount to 18 g a day.

Free radicals These highly reactive molecules can cause damage to cell walls and DNA (the genetic material found within cells). They are believed to be involved in the development of heart disease, some cancers and premature ageing. Free radicals are produced naturally by the body in the course of everyday life, but certain factors, such as cigarette smoke, pollution and over-exposure to sunlight, can accelerate their production.

Gluten A protein found in wheat and, to a lesser degree, in rye, barley and oats, but not in corn (maize) or rice. People with *coeliac disease* have a sensitivity to gluten and need to eliminate all gluten-containing foods, such as bread, pasta, cakes and biscuits, from their diet.

Glycaemic Index (GI) This is used to measure the rate at which carbohydrate foods are digested and converted into sugar (glucose) to raise blood sugar levels and provide energy. Foods with a high GI are quickly broken down and offer an immediate energy fix, while those with a lower GI are absorbed more slowly, making you feel full for longer and helping to keep blood sugar levels constant. High-GI foods include table sugar, honey, mashed potatoes and watermelon. Low-GI foods include pulses, wholewheat cereals, apples, cherries, dried apricots, pasta and oats.

Glycogen This is one of the 2 forms in which energy from carbohydrates is made available for use by the body (the other is *glucose*). Whereas glucose is converted quickly from carbohydrates and made available in the blood for a fast energy fix, glycogen is stored in the liver and muscles to fuel longer-term energy needs. When the body has used up its immediate supply of glucose, the stored glycogen is broken down into glucose to continue supplying energy.

Minerals These inorganic substances perform a wide range of vital functions in the body. The *macrominerals* – calcium, chloride, magnesium, potassium, phosphorus and sodium – are needed in relatively large quantities, whereas much smaller amounts are required of the remainder, called *microminerals*. Some microminerals (selenium, magnesium and iodine, for example) are needed in such tiny amounts that they are known as *'trace elements'*.

There are important differences in the body's ability to absorb minerals from different foods, and this can be affected by the presence of other substances. For example, oxalic acid, present in spinach, interferes with the absorption of much of the iron and calcium spinach contains.
• *Calcium* is essential for the development of strong bones and teeth. It also plays an important role in blood clotting. Good sources include dairy products, canned fish (eaten with their bones) and dark green, leafy vegetables.
• *Chloride* helps to maintain the body's fluid balance. The main source in the diet is table salt.
• *Chromium* is important in the regulation of blood sugar levels, as well as levels of fat and cholesterol in the blood. Good dietary sources include red meat, liver, eggs, seafood, cheese and wholegrain cereals.

• *Copper*, component of many enzymes, is needed for bone growth and the formation of connective tissue. It helps the body to absorb iron from food. Good sources include offal, shellfish, mushrooms, cocoa, nuts and seeds.
• *Iodine* is an important component of the thyroid hormones, which govern the rate and efficiency at which food is converted into energy. Good sources include seafood, seaweed and vegetables (depending on the iodine content of the soil in which they are grown).
• *Iron* is an essential component of haemoglobin, the pigment in red blood cells that carries oxygen around the body. Good sources are offal, red meat, dried apricots and prunes, and iron-fortified breakfast cereals.
• *Magnesium* is important for healthy bones, the release of energy from food, and nerve and muscle function. Good sources include wholegrain cereals, peas and other green vegetables, pulses, dried fruit and nuts.
• *Manganese* is a vital component of several enzymes that are involved in energy production and many other functions. Good dietary sources include nuts, cereals, brown rice, pulses and wholemeal bread.
• *Molybdenum* is an essential component of several enzymes, including those involved in the production of DNA. Good sources are offal, yeast, pulses, wholegrain cereals and green leafy vegetables.
• *Phosphorus* is important for healthy bones and teeth and for the release of energy from foods. It is found in most foods. Particularly good sources include dairy products, red meat, poultry, fish and eggs.
• *Potassium*, along with sodium, is important in maintaining fluid balance and regulating blood pressure, and is essential for the transmission of nerve impulses. Good sources include fruit, especially bananas and citrus fruits, nuts, seeds, potatoes and pulses.
• *Selenium* is a powerful antioxidant that protects cells against damage by free radicals. Good dietary sources are meat, fish, dairy foods, brazil nuts, avocados and lentils.
• *Sodium* works with potassium to regulate fluid balance, and is essential for nerve and muscle function. Only a little sodium is needed – we tend to get too much in our diet. The main source in the diet is table salt, as well as salty processed foods and ready-prepared foods.
• *Sulphur* is a component of 2 essential amino acids. Protein foods are the main source.
• *Zinc* is vital for normal growth, as well as reproduction and immunity. Good dietary sources include oysters, red meat, peanuts and sunflower seeds.

Phytochemicals These biologically active compounds, found in most plant foods, are believed to be beneficial in disease prevention. There are literally thousands of different phytochemicals, amongst which are the following:

• *Allicin*, a phytochemical found in garlic, onions, leeks, chives and shallots, is believed to help lower high blood cholesterol levels and stimulate the immune system.
• *Bioflavonoids*, of which there are at least 6000, are found mainly in fruit and sweet-tasting vegetables. Different bioflavonoids have different roles – some are antioxidants, while others act as anti-disease agents. A sub-group of these phytochemicals, called *flavonols*, includes the antioxidant *quercetin*, which is believed to reduce the risk of heart disease and help to protect against cataracts. Quercetin is found in tea, red wine, grapes and broad beans.
• *Carotenoids*, the best known of which are *beta-carotene* and *lycopene*, are powerful antioxidants thought to help protect us against certain types of cancer. Highly coloured fruits and vegetables, such as blackcurrants, mangoes, tomatoes, carrots, sweet potatoes, pumpkin and dark green, leafy vegetables, are excellent sources of carotenoids.
• *Coumarins* are believed to help protect against cancer by inhibiting the formation of tumours. Oranges are a rich source.
• *Glucosinolates*, found mainly in cruciferous vegetables, particularly broccoli, Brussels sprouts, cabbage, kale and cauliflower, are believed to have strong anti-cancer effects. *Sulphoraphane* is one of the powerful cancer-fighting substances produced by glucosinolates.
• *Phytoestrogens* have a chemical structure similar to the female hormone oestrogen, and they are believed to help protect against hormone-related cancers such as breast and prostate cancer. One of the types of these phytochemicals, called *isoflavones*, may also help to relieve symptoms associated with the menopause. Soya beans and chickpeas are a particularly rich source of isoflavones.

Protein This nutrient, necessary for growth and development, for maintenance and repair of cells, and for the production of enzymes, antibodies and hormones, is essential to keep the body working efficiently. Protein is made up of *amino acids*, which are compounds containing the 4 elements that are necessary for life: carbon, hydrogen, oxygen and nitrogen. We need all of the 20 amino acids commonly found in plant and animal proteins. The human body can make 12 of these, but the remaining 8 – called *essential amino acids* – must be obtained from the food we eat.

Protein comes in a wide variety of foods. Meat, fish, dairy products, eggs and soya beans contain all of the essential amino acids, and are therefore called first-class protein foods. Pulses, nuts, seeds and cereals are also good sources of protein, but do not contain the full range of essential amino acids. In practical terms, this really doesn't matter – as long as you include a variety of different protein foods in your diet, your body will get all the amino acids it needs. It is important, though, to eat protein foods every day because the essential amino acids cannot be stored in the body for later use.

The RNI of protein for women aged 19–49 years is 45 g per day and for men of the same age 55 g. In the UK most people eat more protein than they need, although this isn't normally a problem.

Reference Nutrient Intake (RNI) This denotes the average daily amount of vitamins and minerals thought to be sufficient to meet the nutritional needs of almost all individuals within the population. The figures, published by the Department of Health, vary depending on age, sex and specific nutritional needs such as pregnancy. RNIs are equivalent to what used to be called Recommended Daily Amounts or Allowances (RDA).

RNIs for adults (19–49 years)

Vitamin A	600–700 mcg
Vitamin B_1	0.8 mg for women, 1 mg for men
Vitamin B_2	1.1 mg for women, 1.3 mg for men
Niacin	13 mg for women, 17 mg for men
Vitamin B_6	1.2 mg for women, 1.4 mg for men
Vitamin B_{12}	1.5 mg
Folate	200 mcg (400 mcg for first trimester of pregnancy)
Vitamin C	40 mg
Vitamin E	no recommendation in the UK; the EC RDA is 10 mg, which has been used in all recipe analyses in this book
Calcium	700 mg
Chloride	2500 mg
Copper	1.2 mg
Iodine	140 mcg
Iron	14.8 mg for women, 8.7 mg for men
Magnesium	270–300 mg
Phosphorus	550 mg
Potassium	3500 mg
Selenium	60 mcg for women, 75 mcg for men
Sodium	1600 mg
Zinc	7 mg for women, 9.5 mg for men

Vitamins These are organic compounds that are essential for good health. Although they are required in only small amounts, each one has specific vital functions to perform. Most vitamins cannot be made by the human body, and therefore must be obtained from the diet. The body is capable of storing some vitamins (A, D, E, K and B_{12}), but the rest need to be provided by the diet on a regular basis. A well-balanced diet, containing a wide variety of different foods, is the best way to ensure that you get all the vitamins you need.

Vitamins can be divided into 2 groups: *water-soluble* (B complex and C) and *fat-soluble* (A, D, E and K). Water-soluble vitamins are easily destroyed during processing, storage, and the preparation and cooking of food. The fat-soluble vitamins are less vulnerable to losses during cooking and processing.

• *Vitamin A* (retinol) is essential for healthy vision, eyes, skin and growth. Good sources include dairy products, offal (especially liver), eggs and oily fish. Vitamin A can also be obtained from *beta-carotene*, the pigment found in highly coloured fruit and vegetables. In addition to acting as a source of vitamin A, beta-carotene has an important role to play as an antioxidant in its own right.

• *The B Complex vitamins* have very similar roles to play in nutrition, and many of them occur together in the same foods.

Vitamin B_1 (thiamin) is essential in the release of energy from carbohydrates. Good sources include milk, offal, meat (especially pork), wholegrain and fortified breakfast cereals, nuts and pulses, yeast extract and wheat germ. White flour and bread are fortified with B_1 in the UK.

Vitamin B_2 (riboflavin) is vital for growth, healthy skin and eyes, and the release of energy from food. Good sources include milk, meat, offal, eggs, cheese, fortified breakfast cereals, yeast extract and green leafy vegetables.

Niacin (nicotinic acid), sometimes called vitamin B_3, plays an important role in the release of energy within the cells. Unlike the other B vitamins it can be made by the body from the essential amino acid tryptophan. Good sources include meat, offal, fish, fortified breakfast cereals and pulses. White flour and bread are fortified with niacin in the UK.

Pantothenic acid, sometimes called vitamin B_5, is involved in a number of metabolic reactions, including energy production. This vitamin is present in most foods; notable exceptions are fat, oil and sugar. Good sources include liver, kidneys, yeast, egg yolks, fish roe, wheat germ, nuts, pulses and fresh vegetables.

Vitamin B_6 (pyridoxine) helps the body to utilise protein and contributes to the formation of haemoglobin for red blood cells. B_6 is found in a wide range of foods including meat, liver, fish, eggs, wholegrain cereals, some vegetables, pulses, brown rice, nuts and yeast extract.

Vitamin B_{12} (cyanocobalamin) is vital for growth, the formation of red blood cells and maintenance of a healthy nervous system. B_{12} is unique in that it is principally found in foods of animal origin. Vegetarians who eat dairy products will get enough, but vegans need to ensure they include food fortified with B_{12} in their diet. Good sources of B_{12} include liver, kidneys, oily fish, meat, cheese, eggs and milk.

Folate (folic acid) is involved in the manufacture of amino acids and in the production of red blood cells. Recent research suggests that folate may also help to protect against heart disease. Good sources of folate are green leafy vegetables, liver, pulses, eggs, wholegrain cereal products and fortified breakfast cereals, brewers' yeast, wheatgerm, nuts and fruit, especially grapefruit and oranges.

Biotin is needed for various metabolic reactions and the release of energy from foods. Good sources include liver, oily fish, brewers' yeast, kidneys, egg yolks and brown rice.

• *Vitamin C* (ascorbic acid) is essential for growth and vital for the formation of collagen (a protein needed for healthy bones, teeth, gums, blood capillaries and all connective tissue). It plays an important role in the healing of wounds and fractures, and acts as a powerful antioxidant. Vitamin C is found mainly in fruit and vegetables.

• *Vitamin D* (cholecalciferol) is essential for growth and the absorption of calcium, and thus for the formation of healthy bones. It is also involved in maintaining a healthy nervous system. The amount of vitamin D occurring naturally in foods is small, and it is found in very few foods – good sources are oily fish (and fish liver oil supplements), eggs and liver, as well as breakfast cereals, margarine and full-fat milk that are fortified with vitamin D. Most vitamin D, however, does not come from the diet but is made by the body when the skin is exposed to sunlight.

• *Vitamin E* is not one vitamin, but a number of related compounds called tocopherols that function as antioxidants. Good sources of vitamin E are vegetable oils, polyunsaturated margarines, wheatgerm, sunflower seeds, nuts, oily fish, eggs, wholegrain cereals, avocados and spinach.

• *Vitamin K* is essential for the production of several proteins, including prothombin which is involved in the clotting of blood. It has been found to exist in 3 forms, one of which is obtained from food while the other 2 are made by the bacteria in the intestine. Vitamin K_1, which is the form found in food, is present in broccoli, cabbage, spinach, milk, margarine, vegetable oils, particularly soya oil, cereals, liver, alfalfa and kelp.

Nutritional analyses

The nutritional analysis of each recipe has been carried out using data from *The Composition of Foods* with additional data from food manufacturers where appropriate. Because the level and availability of different nutrients can vary, depending on factors like growing conditions and breed of animal, the figures are intended as an approximate guide only.

The analyses include vitamins A, B_1, B_2, B_6, B_{12}, niacin, folate, C, D and E, and the minerals calcium, copper, iron, potassium, selenium and zinc. Other vitamins and minerals are not included, as deficiencies are rare. Optional ingredients and optional serving suggestions have not been included in the calculations.

Index